The
MEDITERRANEAN
SLOW COOKER

The
MEDITERRANEAN
SLOW COOKER

Michele Scicolone

PHOTOGRAPHS BY ALAN RICHARDSON

HOUGHTON MIFFLIN HARCOURT
BOSTON NEW YORK 2013

To Charles

ALSO BY MICHELE SCICOLONE

The Italian Slow Cooker
The French Slow Cooker

For information about permission to reproduce selections from this book,
write to Permissions, Houghton Mifflin Harcourt Publishing Company,
215 Park Avenue South, New York, New York 10003.

www.hmhbooks.com

Library of Congress Cataloging-in-Publication Data is available.
ISBN 978-0-547-74445-2

Book design by Kris Tobiassen
Food styling by Anne Disrude
Prop styling by Betty Alfenito
Cover photograph: Pork Ribs with Smoked Paprika Sauce (page 146)

Printed in the United States of America
DOC 10 9 8 7 6 5 4 3 2 1

Acknowledgments

Sometimes I think I am one of the luckiest people in the world, because I love the work I do.

For this book, I once again relied on the staff at Houghton Mifflin Harcourt. My editor, Rux Martin, as always, believed in my ideas and gave me clear insights and good direction with her ever-present good humor. Kris Tobiassen created the beautiful design for this book, and production editor Rebecca Springer was there to guide it through the process and keep it on track. Publicists Christina Mamangakis and Brittany Edwards and other HMH staff members contributed to the success of this book, and I thank them for their hard work.

A great team worked together to produce the gorgeous photos. With his creative eye and camera artistry, photographer Alan Richardson makes every dish eye-catching and inviting. Anne Disrude, the food stylist, has a knack for presenting food in a natural and appealing way. Betty Alfenito, the prop stylist, sets the stage for the photos with great style and charm. It is always a pleasure to work with this talented group.

Throughout my career, I have always known that I could count on my friend and agent, Judith Weber, for good advice and sensible ideas. Thank you, Judith.

Finally, thanks again to Charles, who through the years has always encouraged and shared it all with me.

Contents

Introduction

A few years ago, I cleared out a shelf in my kitchen to make room for a brand-new slow cooker. Before long I was using it to turn out some of my favorite Italian dishes—rich, meaty ragus to serve over chunky pastas, the unctuous veal shanks known as osso buco, and the creamiest, easiest polenta I have ever made—each as good as the traditional version, but far easier, and no stirring required. When I went on to try my hand at adapting French dishes, I loved how the slow cooker helped me reduce the three-day odyssey of a cassoulet to a manageable weekday meal.

But why stop there? Countries beyond the borders of Italy and France boast similar slow-cooked dishes that may be less familiar, but no less sumptuous, some with colorful stories to go with them. One such dish, Bandits' Lamb, was supposedly created when thieves stole lambs and dug a pit in the ground that they partially filled with hot coals. As the meat cooked slowly in the pit, it turned buttery soft and absorbed the flavors of the herb, cheese, and garlic seasoning—without alerting the shepherd. Another esteemed dish of the Mediterranean, Portuguese Jugged Chicken, is customarily made in a covered clay pot. In the slow cooker, the chicken and its sauce, redolent of wine and herbs, send out clouds of fragrant steam that never fail to draw guests to the table.

The Mediterranean also offers options for hearty meatless meals. Moroccan Golden Vegetable Tagine, named for the cone-shaped pot in which it is traditionally cooked, is a stew of spiced vegetables and fruits seasoned with fresh herbs that makes a warm and satisfying meal served over rice or couscous. Winter Squash and Chickpea Soup is hearty and chunky with vegetables, just right on a cold, rainy night.

Beyond the usual soups and stews, I discovered a multitude of possibilities. I can't resist Spicy Vegetable Eggah. This Middle Eastern vegetable omelet spiked with chile and cilantro is an eye-opening brunch. And fava beans, slow cooked to tenderness in the slow cooker and mashed to a luxuriant puree, make a unique first course or side dish.

Like favas, chickpeas do beautifully in the slow cooker, which simmers them to perfection so that they can be used in such "Out of the Pot" dishes as Chickpea, Roasted Pepper, and Bacon Salad. The slow cooker also does a great job with whole beets, concentrating their sweet earthy flavor and tenderizing them for a delicious pink Turkish Beet and Goat Cheese Dip—great for a party.

When it comes to dessert, there is no reason to abandon the slow cooker. Try my creamy Spanish-style Coffee Caramel Flan or moist Greek Walnut Cake with Cinnamon Syrup. Two-Berry Clafouti is a simple French custard cake the whole family will enjoy, while Italian Cannoli Cheesecake with chocolate chips and a sprinkling of pistachios will win raves at your next dinner party.

No longer reserved for the occasional pot roast, my slow cooker has earned an honored spot in my kitchen. More than that, it's become a carefree way to replicate the secrets of exotic kitchens with minimal effort.

CHOOSING A SLOW COOKER

Slow cookers have come a long way since they were introduced in the early 1970s. The homely avocado green pots of yesteryear have given way to gleaming stainless steel or handsome brushed aluminum exteriors and easier-to-clean removable porcelain inserts.

Every year, manufacturers turn out new models with added features. Some include different-size inserts for small and large batches of food, while others have flameproof inserts that can be used on the stovetop or in a conventional oven. Some models are preprogrammed to cook popular recipes like chili or stew, and others automatically switch from one temperature setting to another.

Despite the new bells and whistles, slow cookers all cook pretty much the same way, and there is a slow cooker model for just about every need and budget. While I can't tell you which one is best for you, I can tell you some of the things that I look for:

» Large capacity. Cookers ranging from 5½ to 7 quarts are the most practical. They can handle a whole chicken or a roast, a large batch of stew or soup, or even a small cake. Leftovers are great for a later meal. *Note: All the recipes in this book are designed for a large, 5½- to 7-quart cooker.*

» A removable insert for easy cleaning and serving.

» A glass lid that allows you to see how the food is cooking without having to lift the lid.

» A heatproof handle on the lid so that you don't need to use a pot holder when removing it.

» A dishwasher-safe lid and insert for easier cleanup.

» High, low, and warm temperature settings. The low setting is best for cooking meats and soups, which need time to develop flavor, while the high setting is good for delicate foods like desserts, eggs, and fish. The warm setting is good for keeping hot cooked foods ready to eat. Don't use a slow cooker for reheating, because it takes too long to bring the food to the right temperature.

» A programmable timer.

» A signal light that shows at a glance when the cooker is operating.

» A beeper that sounds when the cooking time is up.

» An automatic temperature shift to warm when the cooking is done, in case the meal is delayed.

Here are some other features that are nice, but not essential:

» A preprogrammed 1-hour high setting that brings food up to a safe cooking temperature quickly, then automatically switches to whatever setting you prefer.

» An insert that can be used on the stovetop or in the oven for browning ingredients before they are returned to the slow cooker.

» A locking lid so that you can transport the filled pot without spilling.

» A hinged lid attached to the pot.

» A lid with a built-in spoon holder.

» A temperature probe.

» Lines on the inside of the insert marking the volume of the contents.

» An easy-to-read digital display. Note that in the event of a power outage, a digital slow cooker will not automatically come back on when the power is restored. If you live in an area prone to outages, stick with an analog model.

» Extended cooking capability of up to 26 hours.

» A preprogrammed setting that allows you to press "beef stew" or another preset timing for a specific recipe or to set the timer manually.

» Multiple-size or adjustable inserts for large, medium, and small batches of food.

TIPS AND TECHNIQUES

It may be tempting to just toss the ingredients into your slow cooker and walk away, but I promise the result will be far more delicious if you take the time to learn how your cooker works and follow these suggestions.

Timing

» Slow cookers can vary in the way they cook. Cookers manufactured in the past decade or so are preset to cook hotter and faster than older models because of food safety concerns. The capacity of the cooker, the design, and the quantity, temperature, size, and shape of the ingredients can also influence the cooking time.

» To tell when foods are done, use the timing and visual suggestions provided in the recipes. With slow cooking, a little more or less cooking time often does not make a big difference. If you have any doubts about doneness, check that the food has reached a safe temperature by using an instant-read thermometer.

Always measure the temperature of roasts and chicken in the thickest part of the meat or in the center of the pot. Open the cover, stick the thermometer into the food, and quickly close the cover again. Wait a minute or so to allow the thermometer to register the temperature. The USDA recommends the following guidelines for safe temperatures for slow-cooked foods:

Chicken, turkey, and other poultry ....165°F
Pork, beef, and lamb.. 145°F to 160°F
Ground meats, meat loaf, pâté..165°F

Ingredient Tips

» Vegetables, especially roots like carrots, potatoes, and turnips, cook more slowly than meats, so for stews or soups that combine both, cut the vegetables into small, even pieces and place them around the sides or in the bottom of the cooker.

» Chopped onions, carrots, and celery often taste better when they are first sautéed in a little oil or butter.

» Chicken on the bone is less likely to overcook than boneless chicken. For white-meat chicken pieces, leave the skin on to help keep the meat moist as it cooks. For dark-meat pieces, such as legs and thighs, remove the skin for a less fatty dish.

» Tougher, bone-in cuts of meat are generally the best choice for slow cooking. Not only do they hold up better during the long cooking time and turn out moist and delicious, they are also less expensive.

» Trim off visible fat from meats and chicken before cooking.

» Browning chicken is not necessary unless you are trying to jump-start the cooking. Browned or not, the bird will come out looking and tasting pretty much the same.

» Dried herbs and whole spices, like bay leaves, thyme, and cinnamon sticks, tend to become stronger tasting during slow cooking, while fresh or frozen herbs lose flavor. Use less of the dried herbs and refresh them, if needed, by stirring in a little extra near the end of the cooking time.

» Fresh herbs such as flat-leaf parsley, cilantro, and basil add bright flavor without being overwhelming and liven up the color of finished dishes, making food look more appealing.

» When seasoning soups and sauces, remember that store-bought broth can be very salty. If you use it instead of homemade broth, take the salt content into account and taste before adding additional salt.

» Liquid does not evaporate from the slow cooker, so you may need to thicken soups and stews. There are several ways to do this. The easiest is to turn the temperature to high and uncover the cooker for the last ½ hour or so to allow some of the liquid to evaporate. Or you can transfer some of the liquid to a saucepan and bring it to a boil on the stovetop until it reduces and thickens. Alternatively, bring the liquid in the saucepan to a simmer. Then, for every cup of liquid, stir together 1 tablespoon cornstarch or flour and 3 tablespoons cool water until smooth. Stir this mixture into the simmering liquid and cook for several minutes, until slightly thickened. Return the thickened liquid to the slow cooker and stir to combine. Some soups and stews, especially those made with beans, can be thickened with fresh bread crumbs. (Use plain, unflavored bread crumbs from French bread, if possible.) Stir in as much as you need to thicken the liquid and cook for a few minutes longer to blend the flavors.

» Skim off the fat from the surface of cooked foods before serving.

Equipment Tips

» For easier cleanup, spray the insert of the slow cooker with nonstick cooking spray before adding the ingredients.

» For the best heat distribution, fill the cooker only one-half to two-thirds full.

» Try not to open the lid during the cooking if you can avoid it, because a slow cooker loses a lot of heat when you do that. If you open it, add a little extra time—say, 20 minutes per peek—to the total cooking time.

» Before making a recipe that will be cooked in a bowl, a cake or loaf pan, ramekins, or a baking dish, make sure the dish fits in the insert of your slow cooker. The cooker may have the right capacity, but if the dish has a wide rim or handles, it might not fit. Most large cookers (5½- to 7-quart capacity) can accommodate a 6-cup soufflé dish, four ramekins or custard cups, or a 7-inch springform pan. (You can find these at cookware shops or online.)

» A baking rack allows the heat to circulate around the pan or baking dish. You can buy a small rack, if need be, or improvise one by crushing a sheet of aluminum foil into a ring shape and placing it in the bottom of the insert.

» Specially designed heat-resistant cooking utensils, such as large tongs to grip large pieces of meat, a flat-bottomed spoon, or an angled spatula that can reach down into the bottom of the insert, are helpful for slow cooking and can be used on the stovetop too. (You can find them at cookware shops or online.)

SLOW COOKER SAFETY

SLOW COOKERS ARE SAFE. Since a slow cooker uses only about as much electricity as a 75-watt lightbulb, you can leave it on while you sleep or are out. Be aware that the outer surface can become hot, and always clear the area around the slow cooker. Don't plug other appliances into the same outlet, and never use an extension cord.

TEST YOUR SLOW COOKER. If you have any doubts about the temperature of your slow cooker, try this: Fill the cooker one-half to two-thirds full with water. Cover and turn the temperature to low for 8 hours. At the end of that time, check the water temperature to see whether it is in the safe zone, between 185°F and 200°F. Temperatures below that range indicate that the slow cooker is not working properly and may be unsafe to use. If it runs higher than that, adjust your cooking times to compensate.

FOOD THAT IS FROZEN SHOULD BE DEFROSTED before it goes into the slow cooker. Otherwise, it may not reach a safe cooking temperature within the 2-hour time frame recommended to prevent the growth of bacteria.

DO NOT USE THE SLOW COOKER TO REHEAT COLD FOODS. Reheat foods on the stovetop or in the microwave to ensure that they reach a safe temperature as quickly as possible.

USE AN INSTANT-READ THERMOMETER to test the temperature of cooked foods.

IN THE EVENT OF A POWER OUTAGE while you are away, discard the food in the slow cooker even if it looks done. If an outage should occur while you are at home, transfer the food to a gas stovetop or an outdoor grill to finish cooking.

LET THE INSERT AND GLASS COVER COOL before placing them on a cool surface or in the refrigerator or before adding cold water. Slow cooker inserts can crack or break if exposed to extreme heat or cold or a sudden change in temperature.

Most of the ingredients in this book can be found in ordinary supermarkets, in Middle Eastern or halal markets, or on the Web.

Dairy

GREEK YOGURT is thick, rich tasting, and rapidly becoming popular. If you can't find it, drain regular plain yogurt in a cheesecloth-lined strainer set over a bowl in the refrigerator for 2 hours.

KEFALOTYRI CHEESE is a Greek cheese made from sheep's milk. Sharp, firm, and salty, it is usually used as a grating cheese. Pecorino Romano may be substituted.

Dried Beans

Fava beans, gigante beans, chickpeas, and many other varieties are used all around the Mediterranean. When purchasing dried beans, buy them from a source with frequent turnover to be sure of their freshness. Before slow cooking, dried beans must be soaked in cold water to cover by 2 inches for several hours or overnight. Or use the quick-soak method.

TO QUICK-SOAK DRIED BEANS

Bring a saucepan of water to a boil. Add the beans, cover, and cook on low heat for 10 minutes. Let stand for 1 hour. Drain and rinse. Use as directed in the recipe.

Leeks

Leeks, which resemble giant scallions, are members of the onion family. They can be very sandy, so be sure to clean them well. To prepare them, trim off the dark green tops and the root ends. Cut the leeks in half lengthwise and wash them thoroughly under cold running water, rinsing carefully between each layer. Cut the leeks into narrow crosswise slices.

Lemons

Preserved lemons are whole or cut-up lemons pickled with sea salt and spices. They are used as an ingredient in stews or sauces or as a condiment. If you can't find them, substitute fresh lemon zest and juice.

Sausages

www.tienda.com and www.dartagnan.com are good sources for many types of sausages.

CHORIZO is a spicy pork sausage made in Hispanic countries in many different varieties. For the recipes in this book, use a Spanish-style fully cooked smoked chorizo flavored with garlic and paprika. If you can't find it, substitute another spicy sausage, such as kielbasa or linguiça.

MERGUEZ SAUSAGES are thin, spicy lamb or beef sausages from North Africa. The ground meat is mixed with such spices as cumin, sumac, coriander, and crushed red pepper. If you can't find merguez, substitute another hot, spicy sausage.

MORCILLA is a dark spicy sausage from Spain and Portugal. Made from the meat and blood of freshly slaughtered pigs, it is blended with rice, onion, paprika, and other spices. If you can't find it, substitute another spicy sausage, such as fresh or fully cooked chorizo.

Spices

HARISSA is a hot paste or sauce made from a mix of ground chiles and garlic with such spices as cumin, coriander, and caraway, blended with olive oil. It is found in many Middle Eastern markets in cans or tubes. If you don't have it, substitute another hot sauce, crushed red pepper, or cayenne pepper.

PIMENT D'ESPELETTE is a bright red pepper from the Basque region of France that is dried before being used in all kinds of dishes. The flavor is sweet, mildly hot, and a bit smoky. It resembles a fine-quality paprika or a mild chili powder, either of which may be substituted for it. Use it for eggs, sauces, and stews.

SPANISH SMOKED PAPRIKA, which is made from ground dried chiles that have been roasted over oak fires, is the best kind of paprika to use for the recipes in this book. It can range from sweet (*dulce*) to hot (*piquante*). If you can't find it, substitute piment d'Espelette.

SUMAC is the name of both a spice and the bush from which it comes. The bush grows wild throughout the Mediterranean, and it produces dark red berries that are dried and sold whole or ground to a powder. Sumac has a tart flavor and is good on eggs and grilled lamb and in salad dressing and sauces. If you can't find it, substitute a little fresh lemon juice, grated lemon zest, or vinegar.

TURMERIC is a bright yellow spice that comes from a rhizome in the same family as ginger. Best known for the bright yellow color it gives to prepared mustard, turmeric is usually sold as a powder. It has a flavor similar to that of dried ginger and can be used in soups, stews, and sauces. If you don't have turmeric, substitute a little dried ginger.

ZA'ATAR is a blend of spices that is popular throughout the Middle East. Common ingredients are thyme, oregano, marjoram, sesame seeds, and salt, but other herbs and spices may be used. Try sprinkling za'atar on toasted pita bread brushed with olive oil, on hummus, or in salads. A good substitute is a mix of dried thyme, toasted sesame seeds, and salt.

HOMEMADE ZA'ATAR (Makes about 2½ tablespoons)

Crumble 1 tablespoon dried thyme into a bowl. Add 1 tablespoon toasted sesame seeds, 1 teaspoon dried ground sumac, and ½ teaspoon salt and stir well. Store in a sealed plastic bag in the refrigerator for up to 2 weeks.

Tomatoes and Tomato Products

Ripe tomatoes have a short season, but when they are available, I use them both raw and cooked. If I have the time, I like to remove the seeds and skins from fresh tomatoes before cooking with them.

TO PEEL TOMATOES

Bring a pan of water deep enough to submerge the tomato to a boil and drop the tomato in. When the water returns to the boil, count to 30, then remove the tomato with a slotted spoon. Place the tomato in ice water to cool, then cut it in half through the core. Cut away the core. The skin should slip right off in your hand. Squeeze the tomato to eliminate most of the seeds and the excess juice. Chop it and use in sauces or soup.

When good fresh tomatoes are not available, I cook with canned whole tomatoes, tomato puree, and tomato paste. For canned whole tomatoes, I like the long plum or pear-shaped tomatoes best. When I see a new brand, I buy just one can. At home, I open it to see whether the tomatoes are red from one end to the other and tender when cut. Greenish or white color on the ends indicates that the tomatoes were not ripe enough when they were picked, so they won't be very sweet. Hard tomatoes never cook down into a sauce. Two brands with tender tomatoes and a good tomato flavor are Coluccio and La Squisita.

TOMATO PUREE is good for sauces when you want a smooth, thick texture. The puree should have a balanced tomato flavor, neither too sweet nor too acidic.

TOMATO PASTE in tubes is a great convenience, since you don't have to open a whole can when you need just a spoonful or two to add color and flavor. Amore Tomato Paste is double concentrated for a deep tomato flavor and is widely available.

SUN-DRIED TOMATOES come two ways: marinated in oil and seasonings or dry and unseasoned. Either way, I prefer to soak them since they can sometimes be too salty and over-seasoned.

Soups

Soups

Spiced Carrot Soup

MOROCCO

Out-of-season carrots can be pretty dull, but in this recipe, cumin gives them character, while honey and cinnamon coax out their sweetness. A dollop of yogurt adds a creamy finish, and fresh herbs, if you have them, bring contrasting color.

This sunny orange soup brightens any dark day.

SERVES 8

- 1 large onion, chopped
- 2 tablespoons olive oil
- 2 pounds carrots, peeled and sliced
- 2 garlic cloves, minced
- 1 teaspoon ground cumin
- ½ teaspoon ground cinnamon
- 2 tablespoons honey
- Pinch of cayenne pepper
- 6 cups Chicken Broth (page 44), Vegetable Broth (page 45), store-bought broth, or water
- 2 teaspoons fresh lemon juice
- ½ cup plain yogurt
- Chopped fresh mint, cilantro, or flat-leaf parsley (optional)

In a small skillet, cook the onion in the oil over medium heat until tender, about 10 minutes. Scrape the onion into a large slow cooker. Add the carrots, garlic, cumin, cinnamon, honey, cayenne, and broth. Cover and cook on low for 8 hours, or until the carrots are very tender. Let cool slightly.

Transfer the soup to a blender and puree until smooth, or use an immersion blender. Add the lemon juice and taste for seasonings. Reheat the soup if necessary. Spoon the soup into bowls, top with a little yogurt and the herbs, if using, and serve.

"Cooked Water"
(Tuscan Mushroom, Tomato, and Egg Soup)

Peasant cooks everywhere have a version of a meal cobbled together from whatever simple ingredients they have on hand or can forage. It is sometimes jokingly called "stone soup." Tuscans call their version *aquacotta,* or "cooked water," and make it with mushrooms, tomatoes, bread, and eggs. Although it may be peasant fare, it is a meal-in-a-bowl fit for a king.

SERVES 6

- ¼ cup olive oil
- 1 large onion, chopped
- 1 garlic clove, finely chopped
- Pinch of crushed red pepper
- 1 pound assorted mushrooms, such as white button, cremini, or shiitake, trimmed and sliced
- 1½ pounds chopped fresh tomatoes or one 28-ounce can tomatoes, chopped, with their juice
- 4 cups beef broth
- 4 cups water
- Salt
- 6 large eggs
- 6 slices Italian or French bread, toasted
- ½ cup freshly grated Pecorino Romano or Parmigiano-Reggiano

In a medium skillet, heat the oil over medium heat. Add the onion and cook for 10 minutes, stirring often, until the onion is tender and golden. Stir in the garlic and crushed red pepper and cook for 1 minute more. Scrape the mixture into a large slow cooker.

Add the mushrooms, tomatoes, broth, water, and 1 teaspoon salt. Cover and cook on low for 6 hours, or until the vegetables are tender. Taste the soup for seasoning.

When ready to serve, beat the eggs. Drizzle the eggs into the hot soup and stir gently. Cover and cook for 5 minutes, or until the eggs are done.

Place a slice of bread in each serving bowl. Spoon the soup over the bread and sprinkle with the cheese. Serve hot.

Fennel, Leek, and Potato Soup

ITALY

Fennel is misunderstood. First is its name. You will see it in many food markets labeled as anise, which it is not. Perhaps the confusion comes from the fact that both fennel and anise have a licorice, or anise, flavor. While both plants can be used as herbs, fennel is also treated as a vegetable. It has delicate feathery leaves atop thick green stems and a white bulbous base that resembles celery.

Italian cooks serve it raw as a crunchy appetizer, salad, or palate cleanser or roasted or cooked into soup and stew. In this recipe, it is cooked with leeks, which are a nice flavor complement, while potatoes thicken and give creamy smoothness.

SERVES 6

- 3 medium fennel bulbs (about 2 pounds)
- 2 medium leeks (white and light green parts only), thinly sliced and well washed
- 2 pounds boiling potatoes, such as Yukon Gold, peeled and chopped
- 4 cups Chicken Broth (page 44), Vegetable Broth (page 45), store-bought broth, or water
- 4 cups water
  Salt and freshly ground pepper
- 3 tablespoons extra-virgin olive oil

Trim off the green fennel stalks, reserving some of the feathery green leaves for a garnish. Slice a thin layer off the base and discard. With a swivel-blade vegetable peeler, remove any bruises or brown spots. Cut the fennel into narrow strips.

Put the fennel strips, leeks, and potatoes into a large slow cooker with the broth and the water. Add 1 teaspoon salt and turn the heat to high. Cover and cook for 4 to 5 hours, or until the vegetables are very tender.

Let cool slightly, then puree the soup in a blender or with an immersion blender. Reheat the soup, and season to taste with salt and pepper.

Serve hot, drizzled with olive oil and sprinkled with some of the feathery green tops.

Red Lentil Soup

Green, black, brown, and red are just a few of the different colored lentils available. The texture and flavor vary with the color. Pretty orangey red lentils are particularly attractive. They have a tendency to fall apart, making them not so good for salads but perfect for pureed soups like this one. Full of vegetables and seasoned with cumin, cinnamon, and cayenne, this soup is sweet and spicy in every spoonful.

SERVES 6 TO 8

- 1 pound red lentils, rinsed, drained, and picked over
- 2 medium onions, chopped
- 2 medium carrots, peeled and sliced
- 1 large sweet potato, peeled and chopped
- 1 cup chopped canned tomatoes
- 2 large garlic cloves, finely chopped
- 1 bay leaf
- 1 teaspoon ground cumin
- ½ teaspoon ground cinnamon
- ¼ teaspoon cayenne pepper
- Salt
- 4 cups Chicken Broth (page 44), Vegetable Broth (page 45), store-bought broth, or water
- 6 cups water
- ½ cup chopped fresh cilantro, mint, or flat-leaf parsley
- 1 tablespoon fresh lemon juice, or to taste
- 1 cup plain yogurt

Place the lentils, onions, carrots, sweet potato, tomatoes, garlic, bay leaf, spices, and 1 teaspoon salt in a large slow cooker. Stir in the broth and the water. Cover and cook on low for 8 hours, or until the vegetables are tender.

Discard the bay leaf. Puree the soup with an immersion blender or in a blender. Reheat if necessary. Stir in the herbs and lemon juice. Correct the seasonings. Spoon into bowls, top with some of the yogurt, and serve.

Winter Squash and Chickpea Soup

NORTH AFRICA

A big handful of chopped fresh herbs added at the end of the cooking time gives this sweet, mellow soup extra flavor. It may not be authentic, but I like it with the addition of small cooked pasta, such as orzo.

SERVES 6

- 2 medium onions, chopped
- 2 pounds butternut, acorn, or other winter squash, peeled and cut into chunks
- 1 cup peeled, seeded, and chopped fresh tomatoes or canned tomatoes
- 2 cups Basic Chickpeas (page 175), drained, or one 16-ounce can chickpeas, drained

  Salt and freshly ground pepper
- 2 cups Chicken Broth (page 44), Vegetable Broth (page 45), store-bought broth, or water
- 3 cups water
- 2 tablespoons unsalted butter

  Chopped fresh cilantro, mint, or flat-leaf parsley

Place the onions, squash, tomatoes, chickpeas, 1 teaspoon salt, and pepper to taste in a large slow cooker. Add the broth and the water. Cover and cook on high for 4 hours or on low for 8 hours, until the squash is very soft and falling apart.

With a potato masher or an immersion blender, crush or blend some of the vegetables and chickpeas to make a chunky soup. Stir in the butter and taste for seasonings. Serve hot, sprinkled with the herbs.

Chickpea and Lentil Soup (Harira)

This classic Middle Eastern soup is sometimes made with small chunks of lamb, but I prefer it without meat. Turmeric and tomato paste give it a rich golden color, while the butter and cinnamon bring a warm subtle flavor to the chickpeas and lentils.

SERVES 6 TO 8

- 3 tablespoons unsalted butter
- 2 medium onions, chopped
- 4 tender celery ribs with leaves, chopped
- 1 teaspoon ground turmeric
  Freshly ground pepper
- ½ teaspoon ground cinnamon
- ¼ cup tomato paste
- 6 cups Vegetable Broth (page 45), Chicken Broth (page 44), store-bought broth, or water
- 3 cups Basic Chickpeas (page 175), drained, or two 16-ounce cans chickpeas, drained
- 1 cup brown lentils, rinsed, drained, and picked over
  Salt
- 1 cup spaghetti or linguine, broken into 1-inch pieces, or a small pasta such as orzo
- 1 cup chopped fresh cilantro

In a medium skillet, melt the butter over medium heat. Add the onions and celery and cook, stirring occasionally, until softened, about 6 minutes. Add the turmeric, 1 teaspoon pepper, and the cinnamon and cook, stirring, for 3 minutes. Stir in the tomato paste and 2 cups of the broth and bring to a simmer.

In a large slow cooker, combine the chickpeas, lentils, and the remaining 4 cups broth. Add the contents of the skillet, 1 teaspoon salt, and pepper to taste. Cover and cook on low for 4 hours, or until the lentils are tender.

Stir in the pasta. Cook for 30 minutes, or until the pasta is tender. Stir in the cilantro, taste for seasonings, and serve.

Chorizo and Lentil Soup

SPAIN

A splash of red wine vinegar added at the end of the cooking time perks up the flavor of this hearty soup meal of lentils and garlicky chorizo sausage, flavored with paprika.

SERVES 6

- 2 tablespoons olive oil
- 2 ounces salt pork or pancetta, chopped
- 2 large onions, chopped
- 2 garlic cloves, finely chopped
- 2 medium carrots, peeled and sliced
- 2 medium boiling potatoes, such as Yukon Gold, peeled and chopped
- 1 bay leaf
- 1 pound brown lentils, rinsed, drained, and picked over
- 2 teaspoons Spanish smoked paprika (see page 20)
  Salt
- 7 cups water
- 8 ounces fresh chorizo or Italian sausage links
- 1–2 tablespoons red wine vinegar

In a large skillet, heat the oil over medium heat. Add the salt pork and cook, stirring frequently, until slightly golden, about 5 minutes. Add the onions and cook, stirring often, until tender, about 10 minutes more. Stir in the garlic and cook for 1 minute.

Put the carrots, potatoes, and bay leaf in a large slow cooker. Add the lentils, paprika, 1 teaspoon salt, and the water. Add the mixture from the skillet and stir well. Add the sausage. Cover and cook on low for 6 hours, or until the lentils are tender.

Remove the sausage links and cut them into thick slices. Discard the bay leaf. Add the vinegar to the pot and stir well. Taste for seasonings. Stir in the sausage and serve hot.

Summer Minestrone

ITALY

Minestrone is not just for cold weather. I like to make this one in the summer and serve it as the Italians do, at room temperature, with a splash of extra-virgin olive oil. It's great served hot, too.

SERVES 6 TO 8

- 2 cups chopped fresh tomatoes or canned crushed tomatoes
- 4 medium carrots, peeled and chopped
- 2 celery ribs, chopped
- 2 garlic cloves, chopped
- 2 medium onions, chopped
- 2 cups Basic Chickpeas (page 175), drained, or one 16-ounce can chickpeas, drained
- 2 medium boiling potatoes, such as Yukon Gold, peeled and chopped
- 1 large red bell pepper, chopped
- 1 medium zucchini, chopped
- Salt and freshly ground pepper
- 6 cups water
- ½ cup long-grain white rice
- 1 cup chopped fresh basil
- Extra-virgin olive oil
- Freshly grated Parmigiano-Reggiano

In a large slow cooker, combine the tomatoes, carrots, celery, garlic, onions, chickpeas, potatoes, bell pepper, zucchini, 1 teaspoon salt, and pepper to taste. Add the water and stir to combine.

Cover and cook on low for 8 hours or on high for 5 hours, until the vegetables are tender.

Stir in the rice and cook for 30 minutes more, until the rice is tender and the soup is thick.

Stir in the basil and let the soup cool to room temperature. Taste for seasonings. Spoon into bowls. Serve with a drizzle of olive oil and a sprinkling of Parmesan.

Chickpea "Cream" Soup
with Garlic and Rosemary

ITALY

Italian cooks are masters of simplicity, and this recipe proves the point. Just a few delicious ingredients make this rustic and satisfying soup. Serve it as a first course, followed by grilled sausages or pork tenderloin.

SERVES 8

- 1 pound dried chickpeas
- 4 cups Chicken Broth (page 44), Vegetable Broth (page 45), store-bought broth, or water
- 4 cups water
- Salt
- ⅓ cup olive oil
- 2 garlic cloves, finely chopped
- 1 teaspoon chopped fresh rosemary
- 8 slices Italian or French bread, toasted

Place the chickpeas in a large bowl. Add water to cover by 1 inch. Let stand for several hours or overnight.

Drain the chickpeas. Place them in a large slow cooker. Add the broth, the water, and 1 teaspoon salt. Cover and cook on low for 6 to 8 hours, or until the chickpeas are soft.

Drain the chickpeas, reserving the liquid. Puree the chickpeas in a blender, thinning with the reserved liquid as needed, or use an immersion blender. Reheat if necessary. Taste for seasonings.

In a small skillet, heat the oil over medium heat. Add the garlic and rosemary and cook for 1 minute, or until fragrant. Stir half of the mixture into the soup.

Place a slice of toast in each serving bowl. Spoon the soup over the toast. Drizzle with the remaining rosemary and garlic oil. Serve hot.

Farmer's Vegetable Cream Soup

FRANCE

This simple soup is soothing and easy to make with all kinds of vegetables. It is a perfect way to use up whatever vegetables you have, such as a handful of green beans, a red pepper, or a couple of celery ribs. Originally it would have been made with heavy cream, but half-and-half works nicely and is lighter.

SERVES 6

- 2 tablespoons unsalted butter
- 2 large leeks (white and light green parts only), thinly sliced and well washed
- 4 medium carrots, peeled and chopped
- 2 large red potatoes, chopped
- 1 large turnip, peeled and chopped
- 1 medium zucchini, trimmed and chopped
- 4 cups Chicken Broth (page 44), Vegetable Broth (page 45), store-bought broth, or water
- 4 cups water
  Salt and freshly ground pepper
- 1 cup half-and-half
- 2 tablespoons chopped fresh flat-leaf parsley, basil, or chives

In a medium skillet, melt the butter over medium heat. Add the leeks and cook, stirring often, until tender, about 8 minutes. Scrape the leeks into a large slow cooker.

Add the remaining vegetables, broth, water, 1 teaspoon salt, and pepper to taste. Cover and cook on high for 3 hours, or until the potatoes and carrots are tender.

Stir in the half-and-half and taste for seasonings. Spoon the soup into serving bowls, sprinkle with the herbs, and serve hot.

Flageolet Soup

Delicate-tasting pale green flageolet beans are the French accompaniment of choice for lamb stews or roasts. You can buy them online at www.kalustyans.com or in gourmet shops. Paired with leeks, they make a fine soup to serve as a starter. Tangy crème fraîche is a creamy and cool finishing touch.

SERVES 6

- 12 ounces flageolet beans, rinsed, drained, and picked over
- 2 medium leeks (white and light green parts only), thinly sliced and well washed
- 2 tablespoons unsalted butter
- 2 tablespoons chopped fresh flat-leaf parsley
- 1 teaspoon fresh thyme
- Salt
- 4 cups Chicken Broth (page 44), Vegetable Broth (page 45), store-bought broth, or water
- 2 cups water
- Freshly ground pepper
- About ½ cup crème fraîche or heavy cream
- Chopped fresh chives, flat-leaf parsley, or thyme

Place the beans in a large bowl. Add water to cover by 1 inch. Let stand for several hours or overnight.

Drain the beans and place them in a large slow cooker. Add the leeks, butter, parsley, thyme, 1 teaspoon salt, the broth, and the water. Cover and cook on low for 6 hours, or until the beans are very tender.

Let the soup cool slightly. Puree the soup in a blender or use an immersion blender. Reheat the soup if necessary. Season to taste with more salt and some pepper. Serve hot, with a spoonful of crème fraîche and a sprinkling of herbs.

Cream of Celeriac Soup

Knobby and ugly, celeriac (also called celery root) has a delicate flavor that belies its homely appearance. Once you have pared away the bumpy exterior, you will find creamy white flesh that, when cooked, can be blended into silky smoothness. I especially appreciate this vegetable during the winter, when green vegetables are less available.

SERVES 6 TO 8

- 3 tablespoons butter
- 2 medium leeks (white and light green parts only), thinly sliced and well washed
- 2 garlic cloves, chopped
- 1 large celery root (about 3 pounds), peeled and chopped
- 4 cups Chicken Broth (page 44), Vegetable Broth (page 45), store-bought broth, or water
- 2 cups water
  Salt and freshly ground pepper
- 1 cup heavy cream or half-and-half

In a medium skillet, melt the butter over medium heat. Add the leeks and cook, stirring occasionally, until softened, about 5 minutes. Add the garlic and cook for 2 minutes more. Scrape the mixture into a large slow cooker.

Add the celery root, broth, water, 1 teaspoon salt, and pepper to taste. Cover and cook on low for 6 to 8 hours, or until the vegetables are very tender. Let cool slightly.

Transfer the soup to a blender and blend until smooth, or use an immersion blender. Stir in the cream, and reheat the soup if necessary. Taste for seasonings and serve.

Spinach, Pasta, and White Bean Soup

GREECE

Lots of vegetables, pasta, and beans make this soup a satisfying meal. A generous splash of your best extra-virgin olive oil is all it needs, but you can also sprinkle it with some grated cheese if you like.

SERVES 4 TO 6

- 1 cup dried cannellini or Great Northern beans, rinsed, drained, and picked over
- 1 large onion, chopped
- 3 large carrots, peeled and chopped
- 2 celery ribs, chopped
- 2 garlic cloves, finely chopped
- 1 medium potato, peeled and chopped
- 1 cup chopped fresh or canned tomatoes
- 4 cups Chicken Broth (page 44), Vegetable Broth (page 45), store-bought broth, or water
- 6 cups water
- Salt and freshly ground pepper
- 1 cup orzo or other tiny pasta shape
- 8 ounces baby spinach leaves, chopped
- 2–3 tablespoons fresh lemon juice
- Extra-virgin olive oil

Place the beans in a bowl with water to cover by 2 inches. Let stand for at least 6 hours or overnight.

Drain the beans and place them in a large slow cooker. Add the onion, carrots, celery, garlic, potato, tomatoes, broth, water, 1 teaspoon salt, and pepper to taste. Cover and cook on low for 6 to 8 hours, or until the beans are very tender.

Stir in the pasta and spinach leaves. Add a little warm water if the soup is too thick. Cover and cook for 30 minutes or more, until the pasta is tender.

Stir in the lemon juice to taste and correct the seasonings. Spoon the soup into serving bowls. Drizzle each portion with olive oil.

Bean and Greens Soup

Caldo Gallego, meaning "soup from the Galicia region of Spain," is popular in both Spain and Portugal, as well as in Hispanic countries throughout the world. Some cooks add leeks, others use turnips or cabbage, and some prefer beef to pork. Beans, greens, and meat are the uniting ingredients, but you can be pretty freewheeling with your choices after that. This version is a favorite in my home.

SERVES 8

- 2 tablespoons olive oil
- 2 ounces salt pork or pancetta, chopped
- 1 large onion, chopped
- 4 large garlic cloves, chopped
- 2 medium boiling potatoes, such as Yukon Gold, peeled and chopped
- 1 smoked ham hock
- 1 pound trimmed pork shoulder, cut into bite-size pieces
- 10 cups water
  Salt and freshly ground pepper
- 4 cups cooked or canned cannellini or other white beans, drained
- 1 pound kale, collard, or turnip greens, trimmed and chopped (about 4 cups)

In a medium skillet, heat the oil over medium heat. Add the salt pork and cook, stirring frequently, until tender and golden, about 10 minutes. Stir in the onion and cook until tender and golden, about 10 minutes more.

Scrape the onion mixture into a large slow cooker. Add the garlic, potatoes, ham hock, pork shoulder, water, and salt and pepper to taste. Stir well. Cover and cook on low for 8 hours, or until the vegetables are tender.

Add the beans and kale and cook for 2 hours more, until the meat is tender.

Remove the ham hock and cut the meat into bite-size pieces, discarding the skin and bones. Return the meat to the slow cooker. Taste for seasonings and serve hot.

Spicy Chicken and Vegetable Soup

This spicy soup, known as *chorba* in the Middle East, is made with different veg-etables, a variety of seasonings, and everything from meatballs or lamb to tripe or even octopus. I like this chicken version, popular in Morocco. The turmeric and cinnamon give it a slightly exotic flavor and golden color, while the jalapeño adds a bit of heat. You can add more or less to your taste.

SERVES 6

- 1 large onion, chopped
- 2 carrots, peeled and chopped
- 2 celery ribs, chopped
- 1 medium zucchini, chopped
- 1 jalapeño, seeded and very finely chopped (see headnote)
- 2 cups Basic Chickpeas (page 175), drained, or one 16-ounce can chickpeas, drained
- 1 teaspoon ground turmeric
- ½ teaspoon ground cinnamon
- 4 cups Chicken Broth (page 44), Vegetable Broth (page 45), store-bought broth, or water
- 4 cups water

  Salt and freshly ground pepper
- 1 pound boneless, skinless chicken breast

In a large slow cooker, combine the onion, carrots, celery, zucchini, jalapeño, chickpeas, turmeric, cinnamon, broth, water, 1 teaspoon salt, and pepper to taste. Cover and cook for 4 hours, or until the vegetables are tender.

Add the chicken to the pot. Cover and cook for 30 minutes, or until the chicken is tender and cooked through. Remove the chicken from the pot and cut it into bite-size pieces. Return the chicken to the pot.

Taste for seasonings and serve hot.

Chicken Broth

Whenever you buy chicken, save the spare parts, like necks, gizzards, wing tips, even skin, in a heavy-duty plastic bag in the freezer. When you have enough, thaw them in the refrigerator and toss the parts into a large slow cooker with a few vegetables and water. Vary the flavor by using whatever vegetables and herbs you have on hand. Leave the skin on the onion to give the broth a nice golden color. A squeezed-out lemon half adds a subtle flavor. After a few hours of slow cooking, the result will be more than a couple of quarts of a delectable broth that costs next to nothing.

MAKES ABOUT 10 CUPS

3½ **pounds chicken parts, thawed if frozen**

2 **carrots**

2 **celery ribs with some leaves**

1 **medium tomato**

1 **large onion**

1 **garlic clove**

4 **fresh flat-leaf parsley sprigs**

½ **lemon, squeezed**

2 **fresh thyme sprigs**

6 **whole black peppercorns**

2 **teaspoons salt**

12 **cups water**

Combine all the ingredients in a large slow cooker. Cover and cook on high for 4 hours or on low for 8 hours.

Strain the broth and discard the solids. Pour the broth into small covered containers. Chill for several hours or overnight. Discard the solidified fat on the surface.

Refrigerate the broth for up to 3 days or freeze for up to 3 months.

Vegetable Broth

Here is a basic broth made without meat that can be used for soups, fish, vegetable dishes, and wherever else you want to add light flavor. Don't limit yourself to the vegetables listed; you can use other vegetables as well, such as mushrooms, parsnips, lettuce, and scallions.

MAKES ABOUT 10 CUPS

1 large onion

2 carrots

2 fresh or canned plum tomatoes, halved

2 large garlic cloves

1 medium leek, trimmed and well washed

2 celery ribs with leaves

1 potato, peeled

A small bunch fresh flat-leaf parsley

10 cups water

Salt

Combine all the ingredients except the salt in a large slow cooker. Cover and cook on low for 8 to 10 hours.

Let cool slightly, then strain out the vegetables and discard them. Add 1 teaspoon salt, taste, and correct the seasoning. Store the broth in a covered container in the refrigerator for up to 3 days or in the freezer for up to 3 months.

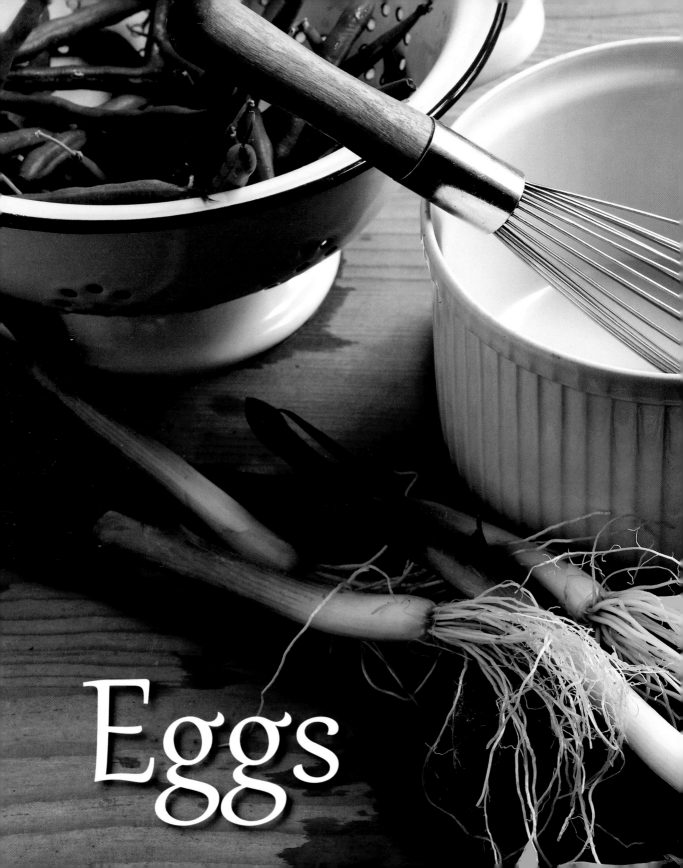

Eggs

Eggs

Spinach and Feta Omelet

GREECE

I love the ingredients in the Greek spinach pie known as spanakopita, so I decided to try them in an omelet. It's delicious hot or at room temperature and makes a good light supper with a tomato and sweet onion salad. Frozen spinach speeds prep time, but 2 pounds of chopped cooked fresh spinach can be substituted.

SERVES 4

- 2 10-ounce packages frozen chopped spinach, thawed
- 8 large eggs
   Salt and freshly ground pepper
- 6 scallions, chopped
- 1 cup chopped fresh dill
- 1 cup crumbled feta or goat cheese

Spray the insert of a large slow cooker with nonstick cooking spray. Place the spinach in a kitchen towel and squeeze it to extract the liquid.

In a bowl, beat the eggs with salt and pepper to taste just until blended. Stir in the spinach, scallions, and dill. Pour the mixture into the cooker. Scatter the cheese over the top, avoiding the sides of the insert.

Cover and cook on high for 60 to 75 minutes, or until a knife inserted in the center comes out clean.

Run a knife around the insert of the slow cooker. Cut the omelet into wedges. Use a spatula to remove the pieces and serve.

Spicy Vegetable Eggah

TUNISIA, EGYPT

French omelets, Italian frittatas, and Spanish tortillas are all in the same family of egg dishes. *Eggah* is the Middle Eastern version. With its spicy flavors, it takes an omelet in a new direction. Serve this with merguez sausages for an eye-opening brunch.

SERVES 6

- 2 tablespoons olive oil
- 1 medium onion, thinly sliced
- 2 medium red bell peppers, sliced
- 2 medium zucchini, sliced
- 1 medium jalapeño or other fresh chile pepper, seeded and finely chopped
-    Salt
- 2 garlic cloves, finely chopped
- 1 cup cherry tomatoes, halved
- 8 large eggs
- ½ teaspoon ground cumin
-    Freshly ground pepper
- ½ cup chopped fresh cilantro

In a large skillet, heat the oil over medium heat. Add the onion, peppers, zucchini, jalapeño, and a pinch of salt. Cover and cook for 12 to 15 minutes, or until the vegetables are tender and beginning to brown. Stir in the garlic and cook for 1 minute more. Let cool slightly.

Spray the insert of a large slow cooker with nonstick cooking spray. Scatter the tomatoes in the cooker.

Beat the eggs with the cumin, ½ teaspoon salt, and pepper to taste. Stir in the cooked vegetables and cilantro. Pour the mixture into the slow cooker. Cover and cook on low for 30 minutes and then on high for 30 minutes, or until just set in the center.

Run a knife around the insert of the slow cooker. Cut the *eggah* into wedges. Use a spatula to remove the pieces and serve hot or at room temperature.

Poached Eggs in Spicy Tomato Sauce (Shakshouka)

ISRAEL

Packed with chunky vegetables, this spicy egg dish is popular throughout the Middle East. The eggs are poached gently on top of a zesty sauce flavored with paprika and turmeric and served in bowls with hot fresh pita bread for a nutritious breakfast, lunch, or supper.

SERVES 8

- 2 tablespoons olive oil
- 1 medium onion, sliced
- 2 medium red or green bell peppers, chopped
- 2 garlic cloves, finely chopped
- 1 small jalapeño, seeded and finely chopped
- 1 28-ounce can tomatoes, drained and chopped
- 1 28-ounce can crushed tomatoes
- 2 teaspoons Spanish smoked paprika
- 1 teaspoon ground turmeric
- 1 teaspoon sugar
- Salt and freshly ground pepper
- 8 large eggs
- Za'atar (optional; see page 20)

In a medium skillet, heat the oil over medium heat. Add the onion and cook, stirring occasionally, until tender, about 10 minutes. Stir in the peppers, garlic, and jalapeño. Cook until slightly softened, about 10 minutes more. Scrape the mixture into a large slow cooker. Add the tomatoes, paprika, turmeric, sugar, 1 teaspoon salt, and pepper to taste, and stir to combine. Cover and cook on high for 2 hours.

Stir the sauce well and taste for seasonings. Break 1 egg into a small cup. Gently slip the egg onto the sauce in the slow cooker. Repeat with the remaining eggs. Sprinkle the eggs lightly with za'atar, if using. Replace the cover and cook the eggs for 10 minutes, or until set to taste.

Spoon the eggs and sauce into serving bowls. Serve hot.

Green Bean and Scallion Torta

ITALY

Something like a frittata, this torta is cooked in a soufflé dish surrounded by water. The steamy atmosphere gives it a tender and creamy texture. Great for a picnic, it slices beautifully like a cake.

SERVES 4 TO 6

> Butter for the dish
> ½ pound green beans, trimmed
> Salt
> 6 large eggs
> ¼ cup milk
> Freshly ground pepper
> ½ cup freshly grated Parmigiano-Reggiano
> ½ cup finely chopped scallions
> 1 tablespoon chopped fresh basil

Butter a 6-cup soufflé dish that will fit in a large slow cooker. Place a rack in the insert of the cooker.

Bring a large pot of water to a boil. Add the green beans and salt to taste. Cook until tender, about 7 minutes. Drain the beans and rinse them under cold water. Pat the beans dry with paper towels. Place them in the soufflé dish.

In a large bowl, whisk together the eggs, milk, and salt and pepper to taste. Stir in the Parmesan, scallions, and basil. Pour the mixture into the soufflé dish.

Pour 2 cups hot water into the slow cooker. Place the soufflé dish on the rack. Cover and cook on high for 1½ to 2 hours, or until a knife inserted in the center comes out clean.

Carefully remove the dish from the slow cooker. Let cool for 10 minutes.

Run a knife around the soufflé dish. Invert the torta onto a serving plate. Cut into wedges and serve warm or at room temperature.

Crustless Cauliflower and Ham Quiche

FRANCE

Cauliflower is my top choice for this creamy quiche, but feel free to improvise with whatever vegetables you have on hand. Try asparagus, mushrooms, peppers, onions, or a mixture of one or more. You will need about 3 cups of cooked vegetables.

SERVES 6

- 6 large eggs
- 2 tablespoons all-purpose flour
- ½ teaspoon salt
- ⅛ teaspoon freshly grated nutmeg
- Freshly ground pepper
- 1 cup half-and-half
- 1 cup milk
- 3 cups well-drained cooked cauliflower, chopped
- ½ cup chopped cooked ham
- 1 cup freshly grated Parmigiano-Reggiano

Spray the insert of a large slow cooker with nonstick cooking spray.

Beat the eggs with the flour, salt, nutmeg, and pepper to taste. Whisk in the half-and-half and milk. Stir in the cauliflower, ham, and ½ cup of the Parmesan.

Pour the mixture into the slow cooker. Sprinkle the remaining ½ cup Parmesan on top, avoiding the sides of the insert. Cover and cook on high for 90 minutes, or until the quiche is just set in the center.

Run a knife around the insert of the slow cooker. Cut the quiche into wedges. Use a spatula to remove the pieces and serve.

Zucchini Flan

ITALY

Cheesy and eggy, this flan has a moist, cakelike texture. Gruyère, Swiss, or Parmigiano-Reggiano are ideal, but I've also made it with leftover chunks and scraps of whatever cheeses I have in the fridge, and it always tastes good. I serve it as a side dish with a stew or roast or as a main dish with a salad.

Once you see how much liquid drips out from the grated zucchini and onion, you'll understand why it's worth taking the time to drain it.

SERVES 4 TO 6

- 2 medium zucchini, grated (about 2 cups)
- 1 medium onion, grated (about ½ cup)
- 1 teaspoon salt
- Butter for the dish
- ¼ cup all-purpose flour
- ½ teaspoon baking powder
- 2 large eggs
- ½ cup milk
- 1 cup grated Gruyère, Swiss, or Parmigiano-Reggiano
- ½ teaspoon chopped fresh thyme

Place the zucchini and onion in a fine-mesh strainer and toss them with the salt. Set the strainer over a bowl and let stand for 30 minutes. Place the vegetables in a kitchen towel and squeeze to remove the excess liquid.

Butter a 6-cup soufflé dish that will fit in a large slow cooker. Place a rack in the insert of the cooker. Stir together the flour and baking powder in a small bowl. In a large bowl, whisk the eggs and milk. Add the flour mixture and blend well. Stir in the vegetables, cheese, and thyme. Scrape the mixture into the soufflé dish.

Pour hot water into the slow cooker to a depth of 1 inch. Place the soufflé dish on the rack. Cover and cook on high for 2 hours, or until the flan is slightly puffed and a knife inserted in the center comes out clean.

Carefully remove the dish from the slow cooker. Run a knife around the soufflé dish. Invert the flan onto a serving plate. Cut into wedges and serve hot or at room temperature.

Mozzarella, Sausage, and Sun-Dried Tomato Bread Pudding

ITALY

Whether served for a special brunch or an impromptu supper, this savory bread pudding is a surefire hit. It has all the flavors usually associated with a good southern Italian-style baked pasta, but without the work. For a bigger cheese flavor, try it with provolone instead of mozzarella.

SERVES 6

¾ cup sun-dried tomatoes, dry-packed or in oil

2 tablespoons olive oil

1 large onion, chopped

3 sweet Italian pork or turkey sausages

6 cups 1-inch cubes day-old Italian bread, lightly toasted

5 large eggs

2 cups milk

Salt and freshly ground pepper

8 ounces mozzarella or provolone cheese, chopped (about 1 cup)

Spray the insert of a large slow cooker with nonstick cooking spray.

Place the sun-dried tomatoes in a small bowl with warm water to cover. Let stand for 10 minutes. Drain well and chop the tomatoes.

In a medium skillet, heat the oil over medium heat. Add the onion and cook, stirring often, until softened, about 5 minutes. Crumble the sausages into the pan and cook for 10 minutes more, or until the sausage is browned.

Place the bread cubes in the slow cooker. Add the sausage mixture and tomatoes and toss well.

In a large bowl, whisk the eggs until blended. Stir in the milk, a pinch of salt, and pepper to taste. Pour the mixture over the bread cubes. Press the bread cubes down into the liquid. Sprinkle with the cheese, avoiding the sides of the insert.

Cover and cook on high for 1½ to 2 hours, or until a knife inserted in the center comes out clean.

Run a knife around the insert of the slow cooker. Cut the bread pudding into wedges. Use a spatula to remove the pieces and serve.

Seafood

Seafood

Halibut with Cherry Tomatoes and Arugula

ITALY

These tasty fish fillets are good hot or at room temperature. For a delicious summer meal, serve them with potato salad and a glass of chilled white wine.

SERVES 6

- 2 tablespoons olive oil, plus more for the insert
- 1 large onion, sliced
- 6 white fish fillets at least 1 inch thick, such as halibut, mahimahi, or grouper
- Salt and freshly ground pepper
- ¼ cup chicken broth, vegetable broth, or dry white wine
- 1 pint cherry or grape tomatoes, halved
- 2 garlic cloves, finely chopped
- 2 tablespoons chopped fresh flat-leaf parsley
- ½ teaspoon dried oregano
- 2 tablespoons fresh lemon juice
- 3 cups arugula, tough stems removed

Oil the insert of a large slow cooker. Scatter the onion slices in the cooker. Place the fish in the slow cooker, overlapping the thin edges slightly. Sprinkle the fish with salt and pepper to taste. Pour the broth around the fish.

In a medium bowl, combine the 2 tablespoons olive oil, the tomatoes, garlic, parsley, oregano, lemon juice, ½ teaspoon salt, and pepper to taste. Spoon the mixture over the fish.

Cover and cook on low for 1 to 1½ hours, or until the fish is almost done. Sprinkle with the arugula. Cover and cook for 10 minutes more, or until the arugula is slightly wilted. (To test the fish for doneness, make a small cut in the thickest part. The fish should appear slightly translucent.) Serve hot or at room temperature.

Tilapia with Romesco Sauce

SPAIN

Romesco is a Spanish sauce made with roasted peppers, tomatoes, and almonds. It has a gorgeous red-orange color and thick, creamy consistency; the almonds give it texture. I first had this sauce on fish, but it is so good that I now serve it on all kinds of things. It's great as a dip for raw or grilled vegetables, boiled shrimp, and plain sautéed chicken breasts, and it also makes a delicious sandwich spread. The sauce keeps well in the refrigerator.

SERVES 6

- 1 large red onion, very thinly sliced
- 1 cup water
- 6 thick fillets (about 2 pounds) tilapia, salmon, or other sturdy fish
- 2 tablespoons olive oil

  Salt and freshly ground pepper
- 6 thin lemon slices

SAUCE

- ½ cup thin strips roasted red pepper (jarred, drained, or homemade; see page 66)
- 1 large garlic clove
- 1 medium fresh tomato, seeded and chopped, or 1 cup drained canned tomatoes, chopped
- 1 slice French or Italian bread, crust removed
- ¼ cup almonds (with skins), toasted
- 1 teaspoon Spanish smoked paprika or piment d'Espelette (see page 19)

  Salt
- ¼ cup extra-virgin olive oil
- 1 tablespoon red wine vinegar or sherry vinegar

Scatter the onion in a large slow cooker and add the water. Arrange the fish fillets so they are slightly overlapping in the cooker. Drizzle with the oil. Sprinkle with salt and pepper to taste. Place the lemon slices on top. Cover and cook on high for

1 to 1½ hours, or until the fish is just cooked through. (To test for doneness, make a small cut in the thickest part. The fish should appear slightly translucent.)

MAKE THE SAUCE: Put the roasted red pepper, garlic, tomato, bread, almonds, paprika, and ½ teaspoon salt in a food processor and chop fine. Add the oil and vinegar in a slow stream and process until smooth. Taste for seasonings. If the sauce is too thick, add a little water to thin it. (The sauce can be stored in a tightly sealed container in the refrigerator for up to 3 days. Bring to room temperature before using.)

Serve the fish with the sauce.

OUT OF THE POT Roasted Peppers

You can find smoky-sweet roasted bell peppers in jars in most food stores, but for the very best flavor, make them yourself.

There are several ways to roast peppers, but as long as I am taking the time, I like to make a big batch of them at once, so I prefer this broiling method. Extras are great to have on hand. At my house, they go quickly—in a salad with garlic and olive oil, as a topping for toasted Italian bread, tossed with pasta, or layered in sandwiches.

SERVES 6 TO 8

6 **large bell peppers (red are the sweetest, but any color will do)**

Cover a broiler pan with foil. Place the whole peppers on the pan.

Turn the broiler to high. Place the pan so that the peppers are about 3 inches from the heat source. Broil the peppers, turning them frequently with tongs, for about 15 minutes, or until the skin blisters and they are lightly charred all over. Do not let them burn.

Transfer the peppers to a large heatproof bowl. Cover the bowl and let the peppers cool completely.

Cut the peppers in half and drain the juices into a bowl. Scrape out the seeds and peel off the skin. Discard the seeds, stems, and skin.

Cut the peppers into strips. Strain the juices over the peppers. Store in a tightly sealed container in the refrigerator for up to 3 days or in the freezer for up to 3 months.

Halibut with Tahini Sauce

MIDDLE EAST

A paste made from sesame seeds, tahini is something like peanut butter. The most familiar use for tahini is in dips like hummus, but here it becomes a smooth and creamy sauce for fish. You can make the sauce several days before serving it, and any leftovers are good as a dip for vegetables or as a sauce for fried meatballs or grilled lamb. Tahini is widely available in cans or jars in both supermarkets and Middle Eastern stores. Store it in the refrigerator.

SERVES 6

- 4 scallions, thinly sliced
- 1 lemon, thinly sliced and seeds removed
- 1¼ cups water
- 6 thick white fish steaks (about 2 pounds), such as halibut, mahimahi, or grouper
- 2 tablespoons olive oil
- Salt and freshly ground pepper
- ⅓ cup tahini, stirred before measuring
- 2 tablespoons fresh lemon juice
- 1 large garlic clove, minced
- Pinch of cayenne pepper
- 2 tablespoons chopped fresh cilantro or flat-leaf parsley

Scatter the scallions in a large slow cooker. Top with half of the lemon slices. Add 1 cup of the water. Brush the fish with the oil and sprinkle it with salt and pepper to taste. Place the fish in the slow cooker and top with the remaining lemon slices. Cover and cook on low for 1 to 1½ hours, or until the fish is just cooked through. (To test for doneness, make a small cut in the thickest part. The fish should appear slightly translucent.)

While the fish is cooking, combine the tahini, the remaining ¼ cup water, lemon juice, garlic, cayenne, and salt to taste in a blender or food processor. Blend until smooth. Taste for seasonings and add more water if needed to make a creamy sauce.

When the fish is done, remove it from the cooker with a slotted spoon. Sprinkle with the herbs. Serve hot with the sauce.

Salmon with Peppers and Charmoula

NORTH AFRICA

Charmoula, or chermoula, is a fresh, green salsa that is used on fish, meat, and vegetables or as a dip for bread in Tunisia, Morocco, Algeria, and other countries in North Africa. The seasonings vary slightly from place to place, so feel free to improvise. You'll find many ways to use this delectable condiment.

The lively taste and bright color are especially good with the rich flavor and texture of salmon. Once you add the salmon to the cooker, watch the cooking time carefully so that it does not overcook. Quick-cooking couscous is the perfect complement to the fish, vegetables, and sauce.

SERVES 6

- 1 medium onion, thinly sliced
- 1 large red bell pepper, cut into narrow strips
- 1 large yellow bell pepper, cut into narrow strips
  Salt and freshly ground pepper
- ½ cup water
- ½ cup chopped fresh cilantro
- 1 large garlic clove, chopped
- 1 teaspoon ground cumin
- ½ teaspoon paprika
- ⅓ cup olive oil
- 2–3 tablespoons fresh lemon juice
- 1 thick salmon fillet (about 2 pounds), cut into 6 serving pieces

Scatter the onion and bell peppers in a large slow cooker and sprinkle with salt and pepper to taste. Add the water. Cover and cook on high for 1 hour.

In a food processor, combine the cilantro, garlic, cumin, paprika, and salt to taste. Process until finely chopped. Add the oil and lemon juice. Taste for seasonings.

Place the salmon in the slow cooker. Spread half of the sauce over the fish. Cover and cook on low for 45 minutes to 1 hour, or until the salmon is cooked to taste. (To test for doneness, make a small cut in the thickest part. The fish should appear slightly translucent.)

Remove the salmon pieces with a slotted spoon. Serve with the remaining sauce.

Poached Salmon in Court-Bouillon

FRANCE

Court-bouillon is a French term for a simple broth used to gently poach fish, seafood, or vegetables. It consists of a handful of vegetables and seasonings simmered with vinegar, lemon juice, or wine.

Poached salmon steaks have many uses. Serve them plain with some of the cooking broth, or chill them for seafood salad. My favorite way to serve this salmon, either hot or chilled, is with tzatziki, citronette, or pesto (recipes follow).

SERVES 6

- 1 medium onion, thinly sliced
- 1 medium carrot, thinly sliced
- 1 celery rib, thinly sliced
- 6 whole black peppercorns
- 1 bay leaf
- 1 large fresh flat-leaf parsley sprig
   Salt
- 3 tablespoons white wine vinegar
- 2 cups water
- 6 salmon steaks, at least 1 inch thick
   Freshly ground pepper

In a large slow cooker, combine the onion, carrot, celery, peppercorns, bay leaf, parsley, a pinch of salt, the vinegar, and the water. Cover and cook on high for 2 hours.

Sprinkle the salmon steaks with salt and pepper to taste and place them in the cooker.

Spoon some of the liquid over the top. Cover and cook on high for 30 minutes, or until done to taste. (To test for doneness, make a small cut in the thickest part. The fish should appear slightly translucent.)

Remove the salmon steaks with a slotted spatula. Serve them hot or lightly chilled.

GREECE

Thick, creamy Greek-style yogurt is the kind to use for this cool, refreshing sauce. If you can't find it, regular plain yogurt is fine, but you may want to drain it in a fine-mesh sieve for a few hours to get rid of excess liquid. Small and crunchy light green Kirby cucumbers or the hothouse Persian variety are less watery and have fewer seeds than the big dark green ones, but any type of cucumber will work.

This sauce is also delicious on grilled lamb chops or as a dip for vegetables or pita chips.

MAKES 2 CUPS

- 2 small Kirby cucumbers, peeled
- 1 cup plain Greek-style yogurt (low-fat or nonfat is OK; see page 18) or other plain yogurt
- 1 garlic clove, minced
- 2 tablespoons olive oil
- 1 tablespoon white wine vinegar
- ¼ teaspoon salt
  Freshly ground pepper
- 1 tablespoon chopped fresh dill
- 1 tablespoon chopped fresh mint

Cut the cucumbers in half lengthwise. With a small spoon, scrape out the seeds and discard. Chop the cucumbers finely.

In a bowl, combine the yogurt, garlic, olive oil, vinegar, salt, and pepper to taste. Stir in the cucumbers, dill, and mint. (The sauce can be stored in a tightly sealed container in the refrigerator for up to 24 hours.) Serve lightly chilled.

Herb and Tomato Citronette

FRANCE

Citronette is the French word for a dressing or sauce made with lemon. This version has chopped parsley and tomato, too. You can also use it to dress salad or steamed vegetables.

MAKES 1½ CUPS

- ½ cup extra-virgin olive oil
- 1–2 tablespoons fresh lemon juice
- 1 tablespoon finely chopped shallot
- 2 tablespoons finely chopped fresh flat-leaf parsley
- Salt and freshly ground pepper
- 1 small tomato, seeded and chopped (about ½ cup)

In a small bowl, whisk together the oil, lemon juice, shallot, parsley, and salt and pepper to taste. Let stand at room temperature for up to 30 minutes. Just before serving, whisk again and add the chopped tomato. Correct the seasonings and serve.

OUT OF THE POT *Arugula Pesto*

ITALY

I like the nutty flavor and subtle bite that arugula brings to pesto. The parsley helps to keep the color bright green. Like basil pesto, this sauce is also good on pasta, in sandwiches, or stirred into soup.

MAKES 1 CUP

- 4 ounces arugula, tough stems removed
- ¼ cup chopped fresh flat-leaf parsley
- 3 tablespoons pine nuts or raw almonds without skins
- 1 small garlic clove
- ½ teaspoon salt
  Freshly ground pepper
- ¼ cup olive oil

In a blender or food processor, combine the arugula, parsley, nuts, and garlic. Blend or process until very finely chopped. Add the salt and pepper to taste. With the machine running, add the olive oil and blend until smooth. (You can make the pesto up to 2 hours in advance.)

Hake in Green Sauce

SPAIN

Hake is a mild, flaky white fish similar to cod. It's traditional in this recipe from the Basque region of Spain, but you can substitute grouper, halibut, or another thick, firm-fleshed fillet. Wine, garlic, and parsley make the sauce flavorful.

You may need to adjust the cooking time according to the variety of fish you use and how thick it is. Keep an eye on the cooker so that the fish does not overcook.

Rice or boiled potatoes are all you need to go with the fish, peas, and tasty cooking juices.

SERVES 6

- ⅓ **cup olive oil**
- 6 **garlic cloves, thinly sliced**
- ¼ **cup chopped fresh flat-leaf parsley**
- ⅓ **cup dry white wine, bottled clam juice, or water**
  Salt and freshly ground pepper
- 2 **pounds boneless, skinless hake fillets, cut into 6 portions**
- 1½ **cups frozen peas, thawed**

In a small skillet, heat the oil with the garlic over medium heat. Cook until the garlic is golden, about 4 minutes. Stir in the parsley. Add the wine, a pinch of salt, and pepper to taste. Bring the sauce to a simmer.

Pour half of the garlic sauce into a large slow cooker. Add the fish and sprinkle it with salt and pepper to taste. Pour on the remaining sauce. Cover and cook on high for 45 minutes to 1 hour, or until the fish is almost but not quite ready.

Add the peas. Cover and cook for 5 to 10 minutes more, or until the fish is barely cooked through in the center. (To test the fish for doneness, make a small cut in the thickest part. The fish should appear slightly translucent.) Serve hot.

Chunky Fish Tagine

MOROCCO

A tagine is a shallow pot, usually made of glazed terra-cotta, that is used to make stews, which are also called tagines. The conical lid collects the steam from the cooking juices and returns them to the pot, keeping the ingredients moist, just like a slow cooker. In this version from Morocco, a tomato sauce simmers with spices, onions, and garlic. When the sauce is ready, chunks of firm fish, herbs, and olives are added and cooked just until done so that they retain their fresh flavor. This makes a great meal with fluffy couscous or rice and a cooked green vegetable.

SERVES 4 TO 6

- 2 tablespoons olive oil
- 2 medium onions, finely chopped
- 1 28-ounce can tomatoes, drained and chopped
- 3 garlic cloves, finely chopped
- 3 teaspoons Spanish smoked paprika (see page 20)
- 2 teaspoons ground cumin
- Salt and freshly ground pepper
- 2 pounds firm-fleshed fish fillets, such as grouper, sea bass, or halibut, cut into 2-inch chunks
- ¼ cup chopped fresh cilantro
- 2 tablespoons chopped fresh flat-leaf parsley
- ½ teaspoon grated lemon zest
- 2 tablespoons fresh lemon juice
- 12 small pitted green olives, halved

Drizzle the olive oil into a large slow cooker. Add the onions, tomatoes, garlic, 2 teaspoons of the paprika, 1 teaspoon of the cumin, ½ teaspoon salt, and pepper to taste. Cover and cook on high for 1½ to 2 hours, or until the onions are tender.

Meanwhile, toss the fish with the remaining 1 teaspoon each paprika and cumin. Add the cilantro, parsley, lemon zest, lemon juice, and salt and pepper to taste. Cover and marinate in the refrigerator while the sauce is cooking.

Add the fish and olives to the sauce, spooning some sauce over the top. Cook on high for 10 to 15 minutes, or until the fish is done to taste. (To test for doneness, make a small cut in the thickest part. The fish should appear slightly translucent.) Serve hot.

Fish Couscous

NORTH AFRICA

Traditional couscous is made by rolling semolina flour and liquid into tiny bits, which are then steamed. Instant couscous, the kind found in supermarkets, is precooked and dried and needs nothing more than hot liquid to soften it—no further cooking necessary.

Couscous made with fish can be found throughout the Mediterranean. The aroma of this spicy North African version is tantalizing, and the colors of the finished dish are gorgeous. It truly is a one-dish meal and, despite the spectacular results, very easy to do. Harissa, a spicy hot sauce, is typically served with this dish at the table, but any hot sauce will do.

SERVES 6 TO 8

- 2 tablespoons olive oil
- 2 large onions, chopped
- 4 garlic cloves, chopped
- 1 tablespoon ground cumin
- 1 tablespoon Spanish smoked paprika (see page 20)
- ½ teaspoon ground cinnamon

  Pinch of cayenne pepper
- ¼ cup tomato paste
- 2 cups water
- 3 medium carrots, peeled and sliced
- 1 large red or yellow bell pepper, chopped
- 1½ cups Basic Chickpeas (page 175), drained, or one 16-ounce can chickpeas, drained
- 4 cups Chicken Broth (page 44) or store-bought

  Salt
- 2 cups instant couscous
- ½ cup frozen peas, thawed
- 3 pounds grouper, halibut, tilapia, or other thick white fish fillets, cut into large chunks
- ½ cup chopped fresh cilantro or flat-leaf parsley

  Harissa (see page 19) or hot sauce

In a large skillet, heat the oil over medium heat. Add the onions and cook, stirring often, until they are tender, about 10 minutes. Stir in the garlic, cumin, paprika, cinnamon, and cayenne and cook for 1 minute more. Stir in the tomato paste.

Add the water and bring the mixture to a simmer. Pour the mixture into a large slow cooker.

Add the carrots, bell pepper, chickpeas, broth, and salt to taste. Cover and cook on high for 2 hours, or until the vegetables are tender.

Place the couscous in a large heatproof bowl. Leaving the cooker on, transfer 3 cups of the broth to the bowl with the couscous and stir well. Cover and let stand.

Add the peas and the fish to the slow cooker. Cover and cook on high for 15 minutes, or until the fish is cooked to taste. (To test for doneness, make a small cut in the thickest part. The fish should appear slightly translucent.)

To serve, fluff the couscous with a fork. Spoon the couscous onto a large serving platter. Top with the fish, vegetables, and some of the remaining broth. Sprinkle with the herbs.

Pass the remaining broth at the table, along with the harissa.

Shrimp with Tomatoes and Feta

GREECE

Shrimp cooked in a spicy tomato sauce flavored with oregano and topped with feta cheese is quick, yet impressive enough for a company meal. Serve the shrimp and sauce over cooked orzo pasta or rice.

Feta is Greece's most famous cheese, but there are many varieties made throughout the world. Traditionally, feta is made from sheep's milk, though today a blend of sheep's and goat's or even cow's milk may be used. Tangy and semi-firm, feta tastes great in a salad or tossed with cooked spinach.

SERVES 6

- ¼ cup olive oil
- 1 medium onion, chopped
- 1 28-ounce can crushed tomatoes
- ½ cup dry white wine
- ½ teaspoon dried oregano
- Salt
- Pinch of crushed red pepper
- 1½ pounds medium shrimp, shelled and deveined
- 1 cup crumbled feta cheese (about 4 ounces)
- 2 tablespoons chopped fresh flat-leaf parsley

In a small skillet, heat the oil over medium heat. Add the onion and cook until tender, about 10 minutes. Scrape the onion into a large slow cooker. Stir in the tomatoes, wine, oregano, salt to taste, and crushed red pepper. Cover and cook on high for 2 hours.

Rinse the shrimp and pat them dry. Stir the shrimp into the sauce. Sprinkle with the cheese. Cover and cook on high for 10 to 15 minutes, or until the shrimp are tender and cooked through.

Sprinkle with the parsley and serve hot.

Tuna and Spinach Pâté with Lemon Mayonnaise

FRANCE

Spinach, tuna, and garlic flavor this creamy, smooth pâté. I like to serve it chilled with a dollop of lemony mayo, sliced tomatoes, cucumbers, and baby greens for a summer meal or appetizer. But it's also good served warm, spread on toasted French bread, for a party appetizer.

SERVES 6 TO 8

Butter for the pan

1   pound fresh spinach, cooked and drained, or one 10-ounce package frozen spinach, thawed

4   large eggs

1   5- to 6½-ounce can tuna in olive oil

1   garlic clove

¼   cup fresh bread crumbs

1   cup heavy cream

½   teaspoon grated lemon zest

Salt and freshly ground pepper

½   cup mayonnaise

Fresh lemon juice

Place a rack in the insert of a large slow cooker. Butter an 8½-x-5-inch loaf pan that will fit in the insert.

Place the spinach in a kitchen towel and squeeze to extract the liquid. Place the spinach in a food processor.

Add the eggs, the tuna with the oil, and garlic. Chop the mixture fine. Add the bread crumbs, cream, ¼ teaspoon of the lemon zest, and salt and pepper to taste. Process until smooth, about 1 minute more.

Scrape the mixture into the loaf pan and smooth the top. Place the pan on the rack. Pour hot water into the slow cooker to a depth of 1 inch. Cover and cook on high for 1 to 1½ hours, or until the loaf is firm and a knife inserted in the center comes out clean.

Let cool slightly. Run a small knife around the inside of the pan. Invert the pâté onto a serving plate.

For the lemon mayo, stir together the mayonnaise and the remaining ¼ teaspoon lemon zest. Stir in lemon juice to taste. Serve with the tuna pâté. Store, covered, in the refrigerator for up to 2 days.

Poultry

Poultry

Spiced Chicken with Pancetta

ITALY

Pancetta, Italian unsmoked bacon, combined with garlic, herbs, coarsely ground pepper, and the unusual touch of cloves, gives this rustic chicken dish a unique flavor. Prosciutto or ham may be substituted. Serve the chicken with roasted potatoes.

SERVES 4 TO 6

- 2 ounces pancetta or prosciutto, chopped
- 6 whole cloves
- 4 garlic cloves, chopped
- 3 fresh sage leaves, chopped
- 1 teaspoon chopped fresh rosemary
- 4 pounds bone-in chicken breasts, legs, and thighs (legs and thighs skinned if you like)
  Salt and freshly ground pepper
- ¼ cup chicken broth

Spray the insert of a large slow cooker with nonstick cooking spray.

Scatter half of the pancetta, 3 of the cloves, and half of the garlic, sage, and rosemary in the cooker.

Sprinkle the chicken with salt and pepper to taste. Place the pieces in the slow cooker. Scatter the remaining pancetta, cloves, garlic, sage, and rosemary over the chicken and add 1 teaspoon pepper. Pour in the broth.

Cover and cook on low for 4 to 6 hours, or until the chicken is very tender and coming away from the bone. Taste for seasonings. Serve hot.

Crunchy Mustard Chicken Diable

FRANCE

Foods prepared in a slow cooker usually turn out soft and tender, not crunchy. But one day as I was baking my usual version of this chicken, I got the idea to adapt it to the slow cooker, for those days when I don't have time to tend to it. I love the result: the bread topping is added at the end so that it's crispy, and the chicken is good hot or cold—perfect for a picnic.

For the best results, make your own bread crumbs from leftover bread or use panko, the light, flaky Japanese-style bread crumbs. If you like your chicken spicy, double the amount of cayenne.

SERVES 4 TO 6

- ¼ cup Dijon mustard
- 2 tablespoons chopped shallots or scallions
- ½ teaspoon dried thyme
- ⅛ teaspoon cayenne pepper
- Salt
- 4 pounds bone-in chicken thighs, skinned
- 2 tablespoons unsalted butter
- ¾ cup fresh bread crumbs, made from French bread, or panko

Spray the insert of a large slow cooker with nonstick cooking spray.

In a small bowl, stir together the mustard, shallots, thyme, cayenne, and ½ teaspoon salt. Brush the chicken pieces with the mixture, turning to coat all sides. Place the chicken in the cooker.

Cover and cook on low for 4 to 6 hours, or until the chicken is very tender and coming away from the bone.

Meanwhile, melt the butter in a large skillet. Add the bread crumbs and a pinch of salt. Cook over medium heat, stirring occasionally, for 5 minutes, or until the crumbs are lightly toasted.

Place the chicken pieces on a platter. Sprinkle with the crumb mixture, patting it on so that it adheres. Serve hot or cold.

Spicy Chicken with Green Olives

MOROCCO

A combination of several spices and herbs gives this savory Moroccan-style chicken great flavor. Stir in the olives near the end of the cooking time so that they don't get too soft. Couscous or rice is the perfect accompaniment.

SERVES 4 TO 6

- 4 pounds bone-in chicken breasts, legs, and thighs (legs and thighs skinned if you like)

  Salt and freshly ground pepper
- 2 tablespoons olive oil
- 1 medium onion, chopped
- 2 garlic cloves, minced
- 2 teaspoons freshly grated ginger
- 1 teaspoon ground cumin
- 1 teaspoon Spanish smoked paprika (see page 20)
- ¼ teaspoon ground cinnamon
- ¼ teaspoon ground turmeric
- ¼ cup chicken broth or vegetable broth
- 1 cup small pitted green olives, drained
- ½ cup chopped fresh cilantro or mint

Spray the insert of a large slow cooker with nonstick cooking spray.

Sprinkle the chicken with salt and pepper to taste. Place the pieces in the slow cooker.

In a medium skillet, heat the oil over medium heat. Add the onion and cook, stirring often, for 5 minutes, until slightly softened. Add the garlic, ginger, cumin, paprika, cinnamon, turmeric, and broth and bring to a simmer. Cook for 5 minutes more. Pour the mixture over the chicken.

Cover and cook on low for 4 to 6 hours, or until the chicken is very tender and coming away from the bone.

Rinse the olives and drain well. Add the olives to the cooker and cook for 30 minutes more. With a slotted spoon, transfer the chicken and olives to a serving platter. Cover and keep warm.

Pour the liquid into a small saucepan. Bring to a simmer and cook until slightly reduced. Taste for seasonings.

Spoon the sauce over the chicken. Sprinkle with the herbs and serve hot.

Jugged Chicken

PORTUGAL

Garlicky chicken braised with port wine and tomatoes and slowly cooked in a clay pot is so popular in Portugal that there is a special casserole dish designed for the purpose. A slow cooker is an ideal stand-in.

SERVES 4 TO 6

4 pounds bone-in chicken breasts, legs, and thighs (legs and thighs skinned if you like)

Salt and freshly ground pepper

1 cup frozen pearl onions, thawed

4 ounces prosciutto or pancetta, finely chopped

4 garlic cloves, chopped

2 bay leaves

2 cups canned crushed tomatoes

½ cup port wine (tawny or ruby)

1 tablespoon Dijon mustard

Chopped fresh flat-leaf parsley

Sprinkle the chicken with salt and pepper to taste. Place the pieces in a large slow cooker. Scatter the onions, prosciutto, garlic, and bay leaves on top.

Stir together the tomatoes, port, mustard, ½ teaspoon salt, and pepper to taste. Pour the sauce over the chicken. Cover and cook on low for 4 to 6 hours, or until the chicken is very tender and coming away from the bone. Discard the bay leaves. Sprinkle with the parsley. Serve hot, with rice.

Balsamic Chicken with Capers

ITALY

This tasty chicken is the kind of dish I can put together in no time, since I always have the sauce ingredients on hand in my kitchen. It's inspired by a grilled chicken marinated in a similar sauce that I had in Rome. Serve with rice and spinach.

SERVES 4 TO 6

- ½ cup balsamic vinegar
- 2 tablespoons Dijon mustard
- 2 large garlic cloves, finely chopped
- 1 tablespoon chopped fresh rosemary
- 2 tablespoons drained capers, chopped
- Salt and freshly ground pepper
- 4 pounds bone-in chicken breasts, legs, and thighs (legs and thighs skinned if you like)

Spray the insert of a large slow cooker with nonstick cooking spray.

In a medium bowl, whisk together the vinegar, mustard, garlic, rosemary, capers, ½ teaspoon salt, and pepper to taste. Dip the chicken pieces into the mixture, turning to coat on all sides. Place the chicken in the cooker and pour on any remaining coating.

Cover and cook on low for 4 to 6 hours, or until the chicken is very tender and coming away from the bone. Serve hot.

Chicken Tagine

MOROCCO

Preserved lemons and fresh cilantro add a unique flavor to this chicken and potato stew. Serve it with couscous and green peas.

SERVES 8

- 3 preserved lemon halves (see page 19)
- 1 medium onion, finely chopped
- 2 garlic cloves, finely chopped
- 1 cup chopped fresh tomatoes or canned tomatoes
- ½ cup chopped fresh cilantro
- 1 teaspoon Spanish smoked paprika (see page 20)
- ½ teaspoon ground cumin
- ½ cup chicken broth or water
- 2 tablespoons olive oil
- 2 pounds Yukon Gold potatoes, cut into ¼-inch-thick slices
- 4 pounds bone-in chicken breasts, legs, and thighs (legs and thighs skinned if you like)
- Salt and freshly ground pepper

Spray the insert of a large slow cooker with nonstick cooking spray.

Rinse the preserved lemon halves and pat dry. Scoop the pulp out of the lemons and chop it finely. Reserve the lemon peel for later.

Place the lemon pulp in a medium bowl with the onion, garlic, tomatoes, ¼ cup of the cilantro, paprika, cumin, broth, and olive oil.

Place the potatoes in the slow cooker and add half of the lemon mixture. Toss well.

Sprinkle the chicken with salt and pepper to taste. Put the chicken on top of the potatoes and sprinkle with the remaining lemon mixture.

Cover and cook on low for 5 to 6 hours, or until the potatoes are tender when pierced with a knife and the chicken is very tender and coming away from the bone.

Transfer the chicken and potatoes to a platter with a slotted spoon. Keep warm. If there is excess liquid in the cooker, pour it into a saucepan and simmer it until reduced. Pour the sauce over the chicken and potatoes and sprinkle with the reserved lemon peel and the remaining ¼ cup cilantro. Serve hot.

Chicken with Chorizo, Red Wine, and Roasted Peppers

SPAIN

Chorizo is a smoky pork sausage generously flavored with paprika, which gives it an orangey red color. There are several varieties—the kind to use for this recipe is fully cooked but not dried. It is widely available in supermarkets. If you can't find it, substitute another type of sausage and add some Spanish smoked paprika (see page 20) to the dish.

In this recipe, the sausage infuses the chicken with spicy, garlicky flavor. Serve it with noodles or rice.

SERVES 6

- 4 pounds bone-in chicken thighs, skinned
- Salt and freshly ground pepper
- 8 ounces fully cooked chorizo sausage (see headnote)
- 1 bay leaf
- 2 tablespoons olive oil
- 1 medium onion, chopped
- 1 garlic clove, minced
- ½ cup dry red wine
- ½ teaspoon chopped fresh thyme
- 1 roasted red pepper (jarred, drained, or homemade; see page 66), cut into thin strips (about 1 cup)
- 2 tablespoons chopped fresh flat-leaf parsley

Spray the insert of a large slow cooker with nonstick cooking spray.

Sprinkle the chicken with salt and pepper to taste. Place the pieces in the cooker, along with the chorizo and bay leaf.

In a medium skillet, heat the oil over medium heat. Add the onion and cook for 10 minutes, or until tender. Stir in the garlic and cook for 1 minute more. Add the red wine and bring to a simmer. Stir in the thyme.

Scrape the mixture over the chicken and chorizo. Cover and cook on low for 4 to 6 hours, or until the chicken is very tender and coming away from the bone. Remove the chorizo and cut into thick slices. Return the chorizo to the slow cooker along with the roasted pepper. Cook on low for 30 minutes more. Discard the bay leaf. Sprinkle with the parsley and serve hot.

Chicken with Feta and Tomatoes

GREECE

Oregano, black olives, and feta cheese add a Greek flavor to chicken. Serve this with orzo tossed with the pan juices and a leafy green vegetable, such as spinach.

SERVES 4 TO 6

- 4 pounds bone-in chicken breasts, legs, and thighs (legs and thighs skinned if you like)

    Salt and freshly ground pepper

- 2 garlic cloves, finely chopped
- ½ teaspoon dried oregano
- 1 pint cherry or grape tomatoes, halved
- ½ cup chicken broth
- ½ cup chopped pitted kalamata olives
- ½ cup crumbled feta cheese

Spray the insert of a large slow cooker with nonstick cooking spray.

Sprinkle the chicken with salt and pepper to taste. Place the pieces in the slow cooker, overlapping slightly. Scatter the garlic and oregano over the top.

Add the tomatoes and broth. Cover and cook on low for 4 to 6 hours, or until the chicken is very tender and coming away from the bone.

Add the olives and cheese. Cover and cook on low for 15 to 30 minutes more, or until hot. Serve hot.

Chicken Legs with Sausage, Tomatoes, and Black Olives

ITALY

Chicken and sausages are a tasty combination, and in this Italian-style recipe, they cook in a lively tomato sauce with black olives. Cook some pasta to toss with the sauce in this satisfying dish.

SERVES 6

- 2 tablespoons olive oil
- 6 sweet Italian sausages (about 1 pound)
- 1 medium onion, chopped
- 2 garlic cloves, finely chopped
- Pinch of crushed red pepper
- ½ cup dry red wine
- 1 28-ounce can crushed tomatoes
- 6 whole chicken legs, skinned if you like
- Salt and freshly ground pepper
- 1 cup pitted black olives, such as kalamata
- 3 tablespoons chopped fresh flat-leaf parsley

In a large skillet, heat the oil over medium heat. Add the sausages and brown them well on all sides, about 10 minutes. Transfer the sausages to a large slow cooker. Add the onion to the skillet, and cook, stirring often, until softened. Stir in the garlic and crushed red pepper. Add the wine and bring to a simmer. Cook for 1 minute.

Pour the skillet contents into the slow cooker. Add the tomatoes and stir.

Sprinkle the chicken pieces with salt and pepper to taste. Place the chicken in the cooker, spooning the sauce over the top. Cover and cook on low for 4 to 6 hours, or until the chicken is very tender and coming away from the bone.

If the sauce is too thin, remove the chicken and sausages with a slotted spoon and set aside. Pour the sauce into a saucepan and bring it to a boil. Cook over medium heat until reduced and thickened to your liking. Return the chicken and sausages to the pot, stir in the olives, and heat. Taste for seasonings.

Serve the chicken, sausages, and sauce hot, sprinkled with the parsley.

Za'atar Roast Chicken and Vegetables

MIDDLE EAST

Za'atar, a blend of dried herbs and sesame seeds, is used by cooks all over the Middle East. It is a perfect seasoning for chicken and potatoes, adding its slightly exotic yet warm and tangy flavor to the dish.

The most common ingredients in za'atar are thyme or savory, sesame seeds, and sumac, a lemony-tasting herb. If you can't find za'atar, see page 20 for a recipe.

SERVES 4

- 2 medium red onions, sliced
- 1 pound boiling potatoes, such as Yukon Gold, thickly sliced
- 3 garlic cloves, finely chopped
- 2 tablespoons za'atar (see headnote)
- Salt and freshly ground pepper
- ½ cup chicken broth
- 1 4-pound chicken
- 1 cup cherry or grape tomatoes, halved

Spray the insert of a large slow cooker with nonstick cooking spray.

Scatter the onions, potatoes, and a little of the garlic in the slow cooker. Sprinkle with a little of the za'atar, and salt and pepper to taste. Add the broth.

Remove the neck and giblets from the chicken cavity and reserve them for another use. Trim away any excess fat.

Sprinkle the chicken inside and out with the remaining garlic, the remaining za'atar, and salt and pepper to taste. Place the chicken on top of the vegetables in the cooker. Scatter the tomatoes around the chicken.

Cover and cook on low for 5 to 6 hours, or until the vegetables are tender and the chicken is no longer pink when cut near the bone and an instant-read thermometer inserted in the thickest part of the meat registers 165°F.

Cut the chicken into serving pieces and serve it hot, with the vegetables.

Roast Chicken with Tapenade

FRANCE

Tapenade from Provence, in southern France, is usually made with black olives, garlic, and herbs that are pounded to a smooth paste in a mortar and pestle. But the variations are endless. Capers, tuna, anchovies, walnuts, sun-dried tomatoes, green olives instead of black, and figs are just a few of the ingredients that turn up in today's tapenades. It is readily available in stores wherever condiments and olives are sold, and I always keep some on hand for a quick appetizer on bread or a sauce for fish steaks, lamb chops, or chicken breasts.

Here I've used it to season a whole chicken and potatoes that are roasted in the slow cooker. Every jarred tapenade blend is different, so taste it first and adjust the seasonings to your taste.

SERVES 4

- 2 teaspoons chopped fresh rosemary
- 3 large garlic cloves
- ¼ cup store-bought tapenade
- 2 pounds sliced boiling potatoes, such as Yukon Gold
- Salt and freshly ground pepper
- 1 4-pound chicken

Spray the insert of a large slow cooker with nonstick cooking spray.

Chop together the rosemary and garlic. Stir half of the mixture into the tapenade.

Place the potatoes in the slow cooker and sprinkle them with the remaining garlic and rosemary and salt and pepper to taste. Toss well.

Remove the neck and giblets from the chicken cavity and reserve them for another use. Trim away any excess fat.

Sprinkle the chicken inside and out with salt and pepper. Place about half of the tapenade mixture inside the chicken cavity. Spread the rest of the tapenade over the chicken. Place the chicken on the potatoes in the cooker.

Cover and cook on low for 5 to 6 hours, or until the chicken is no longer pink when cut near the bone and an instant-read thermometer inserted in the thickest part of the meat registers 165°F.

Cut the chicken into pieces and serve hot, with the potatoes.

Chicken with Middle Eastern Pesto

MIDDLE EAST

Italians aren't the only ones who make pesto. Instead of the classic basil and garlic combo, this Middle Eastern version combines preserved lemons, fresh cilantro, and garlic. Here, it is used to flavor a whole slow cooker–roasted chicken with vegetables. Slipping the pesto between the chicken skin and the meat is simple to do with your fingers. The delicious cooking juices are perfect spooned over whole wheat couscous.

SERVES 4 TO 6

- 1 medium onion, chopped
- 1 medium zucchini, chopped
- ½ cup chicken broth
- 2 preserved lemons (see page 19) or 1 teaspoon grated lemon zest
- 2 garlic cloves
- ½ cup chopped fresh cilantro
- 1 teaspoon ground cumin
- 1 teaspoon Spanish smoked paprika (see page 20)
- ½ teaspoon freshly ground pepper
- 2 tablespoons olive oil
- 1 4-pound chicken

Spray the insert of a large slow cooker with nonstick cooking spray. Scatter the onion and zucchini in the cooker. Add the chicken broth.

Rinse the lemons and cut them in half. Scoop out the pulp and discard it. Coarsely chop the lemon skins. Place them in a food processor with the garlic, cilantro, cumin, paprika, pepper, and oil. Process until smooth.

Remove the neck and giblets from the chicken cavity and reserve them for another use. Trim away any excess fat.

Slide your fingers between the skin and the flesh of the chicken to loosen it. Spread the pesto between the skin and the flesh. Place a little of the pesto inside the chicken. Put the chicken in the slow cooker on top of the vegetables.

Cover and cook on low for 4 to 6 hours, or until the chicken is no longer pink when cut near the bone and an instant-read thermometer inserted in the thickest part of the meat registers 165°F.

Serve hot.

Turkey Breast with Lemon, Capers, and Sage

ITALY

Italians often cook veal with lemon, capers, and sage, so I decided to try that combination with turkey, which has a similar texture and flavor. It's a perfect Sunday dinner or a company-worthy main dish. Buttered rice and roasted asparagus with Parmigiano-Reggiano are the ideal companions.

SERVES 4 TO 6

- 2 large carrots, peeled and sliced
- 1 large onion, sliced
- 1 celery rib, sliced
- 3 tablespoons unsalted butter, softened
- 6 fresh sage leaves, chopped, or 1 teaspoon crumbled dried sage
- 1 teaspoon grated lemon zest
- Salt and freshly ground pepper
- 1 boneless turkey breast half (about 3 pounds)
- ½ cup dry white wine or chicken broth
- 1 tablespoon cornstarch blended with 3 tablespoons water
- 2 tablespoons capers, rinsed, drained, and chopped
- 1 tablespoon chopped fresh flat-leaf parsley
- 1–2 tablespoons fresh lemon juice

Spray the insert of a large slow cooker with nonstick cooking spray. Scatter the carrots, onion, and celery in the slow cooker.

Blend together 2 tablespoons of the butter and the sage, lemon zest, and salt and pepper to taste. Loosen but do not remove the skin on the turkey breast and gently spread the butter mixture between the skin and meat, trying not to tear the skin.

Place the turkey breast in the slow cooker. Pour the wine around the turkey. Cover and cook on high for 3 to 4 hours, or until an instant-read thermometer inserted in the thickest part of the meat registers 165°F.

Remove the turkey from the pot. Cover and keep warm. Strain the cooking liquid into a small saucepan. Bring the juices to a boil.

Add the cornstarch mixture to the turkey juices and stir well. Cook for 1 minute, or until slightly thickened. Off the heat, whisk in the remaining 1 tablespoon butter, the capers, parsley, and lemon juice to taste.

Carve the turkey and serve it hot, with the sauce.

Turkey Meat Loaf with Sun-Dried Tomatoes and Mozzarella

ITALY

With sun-dried tomatoes, fresh basil, and cheeses, this meat loaf captures the flavor of southern Italy. It was inspired by one that chef and restaurateur Lidia Bastianich made on her television show *Lidia's Italy*. I don't remember what the other ingredients were, but I loved the idea of adding cubes of mozzarella to the meat mixture, so I came up with my own version. I serve the meat loaf either hot or cold. Keep in mind that once the leftovers are chilled, you lose the luscious meltiness of the mozzarella.

Serve the meat loaf as is or with a tomato sauce such as the one on page 199.

SERVES 8

    1 cup drained sun-dried tomatoes in oil
    2 pounds ground turkey
    3 large eggs, beaten
    ½ cup plain dry bread crumbs
    ½ cup finely chopped scallions
    ½ cup freshly grated Parmigiano-Reggiano
    ¼ cup chopped fresh basil
   1½ teaspoons salt
       Freshly ground pepper
    8 ounces mozzarella, cut into ½-inch cubes

Fold a 2-foot length of aluminum foil in half lengthwise. Place the foil into the insert of a large slow cooker, pressing it against the bottom and up the sides. Spray the foil and the insert with nonstick cooking spray.

Rinse the sun-dried tomatoes under warm water. Pat them dry with paper towels. Set aside a few pieces for the top of the meat loaf. Stack the remaining tomatoes and chop them into small pieces.

In a large bowl, combine all the ingredients except the mozzarella and reserved sun-dried tomatoes and mix well. Add the mozzarella. Moisten your hands in cold water and shape the mixture into an oval loaf slightly smaller than the interior of the slow cooker. Carefully place the loaf into the cooker, on top of the foil. Press the reserved tomato pieces into the top in a decorative pattern. (A flower looks nice.)

Cover and cook on high for 3 to 4 hours, or until an instant-read thermometer inserted in the center of the loaf registers 165°F.

Carefully lift the meat loaf out of the slow cooker, using the ends of the foil as handles. Slide the meat loaf onto a serving platter. Cut into slices and serve hot.

Duck Ragu

ITALY

Duck legs give a slightly gamy flavor to this thick, rich ragu. I like to serve it on pappardelle, wide ribbons of fresh egg pasta, but fettuccine is fine too. Or instead of the pasta, serve it with Polenta with Herbs (page 164). And don't forget a good bottle of Italian red wine, such as Barolo.

SERVES 8

- 2 tablespoons olive oil
- 4 ounces pancetta, chopped
- 6 whole duck legs and thighs, skinned
- Salt and freshly ground pepper
- 4 medium carrots, peeled and chopped
- 2 celery ribs, chopped
- 1 large red onion, chopped
- 2 tablespoons all-purpose flour
- 1 cup dry red wine
- ½ cup tomato paste
- Pinch of ground cloves
- 2 cups Chicken Broth (page 44) or store-bought broth

In a large skillet, heat the oil over medium heat. Add the pancetta and cook, stirring often, until nicely browned, about 10 minutes. Transfer the pancetta to a large slow cooker.

Pat the duck legs dry with paper towels. Sprinkle them all over with salt and pepper. Add the duck legs to the skillet, in batches if necessary, and cook until browned on all sides, about 15 minutes in all. Transfer the duck to the cooker.

Add the carrots, celery, and onion to the skillet. Cook for 10 minutes, or until the vegetables are tender. Stir in the flour and cook for 1 minute. Add the wine, tomato paste, and cloves and cook, scraping the bottom of the pan, until the liquid comes to a boil.

Scrape the mixture into the slow cooker. Add the broth. Cover and cook on low for 4 to 5 hours, or until the duck is very tender and coming away from the bone.

Transfer the duck legs to a cutting board, but leave the cooker on. Remove the meat from the bones and cut it into small dice. Discard the bones.

Return the duck meat to the sauce and reheat. Serve hot.

Beef and Veal

Beef and Veal

Porcini Braised Beef

ITALY

Dried porcini mushrooms make a perfect gravy for simmering this beef pot roast. Porcini, known as *cèpes* in France, are my favorite, but you can substitute another type of dried mushroom. Serve the sliced beef with potatoes mashed with Parmigiano-Reggiano or with buttered broad egg noodles.

SERVES 6 TO 8

- ⅓ **cup all-purpose flour**
- **Salt and freshly ground pepper**
- 1 **boneless beef chuck or bottom round roast (about 3½ pounds)**
- 3 **tablespoons olive oil**
- 2 **medium red onions, finely chopped**
- ½ **cup dry red wine**
- 1 **cup beef broth**
- ½ **cup dried porcini, shiitake, or other mushrooms**
- 2 **tablespoons tomato paste**

Combine the flour with salt and pepper to taste. Spread the mixture on a piece of wax paper and roll the beef in the flour.

In a large, heavy skillet, heat the oil over medium-high heat. Add the beef and brown it on all sides, about 20 minutes total. Place the beef in a large slow cooker. Add the onions to the skillet and cook, stirring often, for 10 minutes, or until softened. Add the wine and bring it to a simmer. Stir in the broth, mushrooms, tomato paste, and salt and pepper to taste. Bring the mixture to a simmer.

Pour the mixture over the beef. Cover and cook on low for 8 hours, or until the meat is tender when pierced with a fork.

Transfer the meat to a platter. Skim the fat from the surface of the sauce. Taste for seasonings. Slice the meat and pour on the sauce. Serve hot.

Beef Stew with Cinnamon and Tiny Onions

GREECE

A small amount of ground cinnamon and a splash of vinegar add an elusive flavor to this Greek-style beef stew. It looks and tastes familiar but is just different enough to make it special.

For a lighter alternative to potatoes mashed with butter, I serve the stew with cauliflower and potatoes mashed with extra-virgin olive oil.

SERVES 6 TO 8

- 3 tablespoons olive oil
- 3½ pounds beef chuck, cut into 2-inch pieces
  Salt and freshly ground pepper
- 1 large onion, chopped
- 2 garlic cloves, very finely chopped
- 24 pearl onions, trimmed, or frozen pearl onions, thawed
- ½ cup dry red wine
- ¼ cup red wine vinegar
- 1 28-ounce can tomato puree
- 1 bay leaf
- ½ teaspoon ground cinnamon

In a large, heavy skillet, heat the oil over medium-high heat. Pat the beef dry with paper towels. Add the beef in batches, without crowding the pan. Brown the beef well on all sides, about 15 minutes per batch. With a slotted spoon, transfer the beef to a large slow cooker. Sprinkle with salt and pepper to taste.

Add the chopped onion to the skillet and cook, stirring often, until softened, about 10 minutes. Stir in the garlic and cook for 1 minute more. Stir in the pearl onions, wine, and vinegar. Bring the liquid to a simmer. Pour the mixture into the slow cooker. Add the tomato puree, bay leaf, and cinnamon and stir well.

Cover and cook on low for 6 to 8 hours, or until the beef is very tender. Discard the bay leaf. Serve hot.

Shredded Beef with Peppers

SPAIN

This dish is called *ropa vieja*, meaning "old clothes," in Spain, for the look of the shredded beef. It's a great way to tenderize a tough cut like flank steak or brisket. Rice is the traditional accompaniment, and I also like to serve the stew with chickpeas. For a spicy kick, serve it with hot sauce.

SERVES 6

- 2 celery ribs, chopped
- 2 garlic cloves, minced
- 1 large onion, finely chopped
- 1 large red pepper, cut into thin strips
- 1 large green pepper, cut into thin strips
- 1 teaspoon ground cumin
- ½ teaspoon dried oregano
- 1 28-ounce can crushed tomatoes
- ½ cup water
- 3 pounds flank steak or brisket, cut into large chunks
  Salt and freshly ground pepper
- 1 cup small pimiento-stuffed green olives, drained and rinsed

In a large slow cooker, combine the celery, garlic, onion, peppers, cumin, and oregano. Add the crushed tomatoes and water and stir well.

Sprinkle the beef with salt and pepper to taste. Place the pieces in the slow cooker, spooning some of the sauce over the top. Cover and cook on low for 6 to 7 hours, or until the meat is tender.

Remove the meat from the slow cooker but leave the cooker on. With two forks, shred the meat into bite-size pieces. Return the meat to the slow cooker. Taste for seasonings. Stir in the olives and cook for 30 minutes more to blend the flavors. Serve hot.

Shredded Beef Ragu

ITALY

In Italy, pot roast or stew is called *stracotto*, meaning "overcooked." This saucy brisket is so soft that it shreds easily and makes a perfect topping for pasta, rice, or polenta.

MAKES ABOUT 8 CUPS; ENOUGH FOR 2 POUNDS PASTA, SERVING 8

2	tablespoons olive oil
2	ounces pancetta, chopped
2	large red onions, chopped
2	medium carrots, peeled and chopped
2	celery ribs, chopped
6	garlic cloves, chopped
½	cup dry red wine
1	28-ounce can crushed tomatoes
1	cup beef broth
2	bay leaves
	Salt and freshly ground pepper
1	2½-pound beef brisket

In a large skillet, heat the oil over medium heat. Add the pancetta and cook, stirring often, until golden, about 10 minutes. Add the onions, carrots, celery, and garlic and cook, stirring frequently, until the vegetables are softened, about 10 minutes. Add the wine and bring it to a simmer. Scrape the mixture into a large slow cooker.

Add the tomatoes, broth, bay leaves, and salt and pepper to taste. Stir well. Add the beef, spooning some of the sauce over the top. Cover and cook on low for 8 to 10 hours, or until the beef is fork-tender.

Carefully transfer the beef to a cutting board but leave the slow cooker on. Discard the bay leaves. With two forks, shred the meat into bite-size pieces. Return the meat to the sauce to reheat. Serve hot.

Pot-au-Feu (Beef and Vegetables)

FRANCE

The French call this boiled beef dinner *pot-au-feu,* meaning "pot on the fire," because of the long, slow cooking time. The broth makes a perfect first course, while the beef and vegetables are served as a second course with a pot of mustard, prepared horseradish, and cornichons, the tiny French pickles. Follow with a platter of cheese and a baguette for a great French country meal.

SERVES 6

- 4 whole garlic cloves
- 4 medium carrots, peeled and cut into 1-inch chunks
- 6 medium Yukon Gold potatoes, peeled and cut into 1-inch chunks
- 2 medium parsnips, peeled and cut into 1-inch chunks
- 2 medium turnips, peeled and cut into 1-inch chunks
- 2 leeks (white and light green parts only), sliced into ½-inch pieces and well washed
- 3 fresh flat-leaf parsley sprigs
- 4 fresh thyme sprigs
- 1 bay leaf
- 2½ pounds boneless beef chuck or brisket, well trimmed
- 2 pounds beef short ribs or shanks, well trimmed
  Salt
- 10 whole black peppercorns
  Mustard, prepared horseradish, and cornichons

Place the garlic and vegetables in a large slow cooker. Wrap the parsley, thyme, and bay leaf in kitchen twine to make a bundle that you can remove easily. Toss it into the cooker. Place the meat on top. Add salt to taste, the peppercorns, and just enough water to cover the meat and vegetables.

Cover and cook on low for 8 to 10 hours, or until the meat is very tender when pierced with a fork.

Remove the meat and cut it into chunks. Arrange the meat and vegetables on a serving platter. Cover and keep warm.

Remove the bundle of herbs and discard. Skim the fat from the surface of the broth and taste the broth for seasonings. Pour some of the broth over the meat. Place the meat and vegetables in a low (200°F) oven to keep warm.

Serve the remaining broth as a first course, followed by the meat and vegetables. Pass the mustard, horseradish, and cornichons at the table.

Florentine Beef with Red Onion Gravy

ITALY

Mild, sweet red onions form the base of the sauce for this tender beef pot roast. Rather than thickening the sauce with flour or cornstarch, you whirl the cooked vegetables in the blender to make a natural thickener. You will want to serve this with lots of mashed potatoes or egg noodles to take full advantage of the abundant, flavorful gravy.

This is a great dish for entertaining, since it can be cooked days ahead of serving, then sliced and reheated in the sauce on the stovetop.

SERVES 6 TO 8

- 3 tablespoons olive oil
- ½ cup chopped pancetta
- 4 medium red onions, thinly sliced
- 2 medium carrots, peeled and sliced
- 1 celery rib, sliced
- 2 garlic cloves, finely chopped
  Salt
- 1 cup beef broth
- 1 cup dry red wine
- 1 cup tomato puree
- 1 4-pound beef brisket, trimmed
  Freshly ground pepper
- 2 tablespoons chopped fresh flat-leaf parsley

In a large skillet, heat the oil over medium heat. Add the pancetta and cook, stirring often, for 5 minutes, or until golden. Add the onions, carrots, celery, garlic, salt to taste, and ½ cup of the broth. Cover and cook, stirring occasionally, until the vegetables are softened, about 20 minutes. Add the wine and bring to a simmer.

Pour the contents of the skillet into a large slow cooker. Stir in the remaining ½ cup broth and the tomato puree. Sprinkle the beef with salt and pepper to taste. Add the beef to the slow cooker, spooning some of the sauce and vegetables over the top. Cover and cook on low for 7 to 8 hours, or until the meat is fork-tender.

Transfer the meat to a platter. Cover and keep warm. Skim the fat from the surface of the sauce. Pour the sauce and vegetables into a blender and blend until smooth. Add salt and pepper to taste. Reheat if necessary.

Slice the beef across the grain and pour the sauce over it. Sprinkle with the parsley and serve hot.

Steak with Pizzaiola Sauce

ITALY

When I was young, my mom didn't have a slow cooker, but she made this go-to dish for us often because she could whip it up in a hurry and leave it to simmer on the stovetop.

Cooked at a leisurely pace in the slow cooker, the tough beef turns buttery soft. Since the garlic and oregano tend to mellow out during the cooking, I add more at the end so that the bright flavors of the garlic, herbs, and hot pepper shine through. There's nothing subtle about this dish!

I cook the steaks in a generous amount of tomato sauce so that there will be plenty to sauce cooked spaghetti. We always had the spaghetti as a first course, followed by the beef and a green salad.

SERVES 8

3 pounds small boneless beef steaks, such as chuck steaks

Salt and freshly ground pepper

½ cup all-purpose flour

3 tablespoons olive oil

2 28-ounce cans crushed tomatoes

½ cup water

2 tablespoons finely chopped garlic

1 teaspoon dried oregano

Crushed red pepper

Hot cooked spaghetti

Pat the steaks dry with paper towels and sprinkle with salt and pepper to taste. Dredge the steaks lightly in the flour.

In a large, heavy skillet, heat the oil over medium-high heat. Add the steaks to the pan. Cook until the steaks are browned, about 3 minutes on each side. Transfer the steaks to a large slow cooker, overlapping the pieces slightly.

In a large bowl, stir together the tomatoes, water, 1 tablespoon of the garlic, ½ teaspoon of the oregano, a pinch of crushed red pepper, and salt to taste. Pour the sauce over the steaks. Cover and cook on low for 6 to 8 hours, or until the steaks are very tender.

Stir the remaining 1 tablespoon garlic, the remaining ½ teaspoon oregano, and another pinch of crushed red pepper into the sauce. Taste for seasonings.

Remove the steaks from the slow cooker and place them on a warm platter. Serve hot, with the spaghetti topped with the tomato sauce.

Beef Short Ribs with Carrots and Black Olives

FRANCE

Beefy short ribs are an ideal substitute for the bull meat that is typically used to make this stew in southern France. Be sure to use a flavorful olive, such as the tiny niçoise olives or the wrinkly black olives from Nyons. Add them near the end of the cooking time so that they don't get mushy.

SERVES 6 TO 8

2 tablespoons olive oil

4½ pounds bone-in beef short ribs, well trimmed

8 medium carrots, peeled and cut into ½-inch diagonal slices

Salt and freshly ground pepper

2 medium onions, sliced

6 garlic cloves, finely chopped

2 cups dry white wine

1 bay leaf

2 fresh thyme sprigs

1 cup pitted black olives (see headnote)

In a large, heavy skillet, heat the oil over medium-high heat. Pat the ribs dry with paper towels and cook them in batches until nicely browned on all sides, about 30 minutes total.

Place the carrots in a large slow cooker. Place the ribs on top. Sprinkle with salt and pepper to taste.

Pour off any excess fat from the skillet. Add the onions and cook, stirring occasionally, until they are tender, about 10 minutes. Stir in the garlic and cook for 1 minute more. Add the wine, bay leaf, and thyme and bring the liquid to a simmer. Pour the contents of the skillet into the slow cooker.

Cover and cook on low for 7 to 8 hours, or until the meat is very tender and pulling away from the bones. Add the olives and cook for 30 minutes more.

Transfer the ribs to a serving dish. Discard any loose bones, the bay leaf, and the thyme. Cover and keep warm. Skim the fat from the surface of the sauce. Transfer the sauce to a small pan and bring it to a simmer over high heat. Cook until the liquid is slightly reduced, about 10 minutes. Taste for seasonings. Pour the sauce over the ribs and serve hot.

Rioja Short Ribs with Chorizo

SPAIN

Made from ground pork, chorizo sausage is seasoned with smoky paprika and garlic. In this recipe, the sausage meat is removed from the casing to add flavor to tender beef short ribs simmered in a tomato sauce with robust Rioja wine and a dash of nutty sherry vinegar. All it needs is some fluffy cooked rice.

SERVES 6

- 2 tablespoons olive oil
- 3½ pounds bone-in beef short ribs, well trimmed
  Salt and freshly ground pepper
- 4 ounces fully cooked chorizo sausage, casings removed
- 1 medium onion, finely chopped
- 4 medium carrots, peeled and sliced
- 1 teaspoon piment d'Espelette or Spanish smoked paprika (see page 20)
- 4 garlic cloves, finely chopped
- 1 bay leaf
- 1 28-ounce can tomatoes, drained and chopped
- 1 cup Rioja or other dry red wine
- 1 tablespoon sherry vinegar
- 2 tablespoons chopped fresh flat-leaf parsley

In a large, heavy skillet, heat the oil over medium-high heat. Pat the ribs dry with paper towels and cook in batches until nicely browned on all sides, about 30 minutes total. Transfer the ribs to a large slow cooker and sprinkle with salt and pepper to taste.

Discard all but 1 tablespoon of the fat in the skillet and reduce the heat to medium. Add the chorizo, onion, and carrots. Cook, stirring occasionally, until the vegetables are softened and the chorizo is lightly browned, about 10 minutes. Add the piment d'Espelette, garlic, bay leaf, tomatoes, and wine. Bring to a simmer and cook for 1 minute. Pour the sauce over the ribs. Cover and cook on low for 7 to 8 hours, or until the ribs are very tender.

Remove the ribs from the slow cooker. Discard any loose bones and the bay leaf. Cover and keep warm.

Skim the fat from the surface of the sauce. Stir in the vinegar and add salt and pepper to taste. Pour the sauce over the ribs. Sprinkle with the parsley and serve hot.

Beef Short Ribs with Mustard and Red Wine

FRANCE

Mustard is one of the seasonings that I particularly like to use in slow-cooked recipes, since it adds flavor that holds up well during the long cooking time. These short ribs are a good example. As the meat melts away from the bone, the mustard, seasonings, and red wine form a delicious sauce to spoon over the top.

SERVES 4 TO 6

- 2 tablespoons olive oil
- 4 pounds bone-in beef short ribs, well trimmed
  Salt and freshly ground pepper
- 2 large shallots, chopped
- 2 garlic cloves, finely chopped
- 1 cup dry red wine or beef broth
- 3 tablespoons coarse-grain mustard
- 3 tablespoons tomato paste
- 1 fresh thyme sprig

In a large, heavy skillet, heat the oil over medium-high heat. Pat the short ribs dry with paper towels and cook in batches until nicely browned on all sides, about 30 minutes total. Transfer the beef to a large slow cooker and sprinkle with salt and pepper to taste.

Add the shallots and garlic to the skillet and cook for 2 minutes. Add the wine, mustard, and tomato paste and cook, stirring and scraping the bottom of the pan, until the liquid comes to a simmer.

Pour the liquid over the beef. Add the thyme. Cover and cook on low for 8 hours, or until the meat is very tender. Remove the ribs from the slow cooker, discarding any loose bones and the thyme sprig. Cover and keep warm.

Skim the fat from the surface of the sauce. Pour the sauce over the meat and serve hot.

Sweet and Sour Meatballs

ISRAEL

When I was a young bride, one of my favorite recipe sources was *The New York Times International Cookbook*. I loved trying the foods from faraway lands that I could only dream about visiting someday. Sweet and sour meatballs were a big favorite then, and I still make the recipe, though I have adapted it to the slow cooker and tweaked it by adding tomato sauce and raisins to the pot.

SERVES 6 TO 8

3 cups All-Purpose Tomato Sauce (page 199) or other tomato sauce

1 cup water

¼ cup dark brown sugar

2 tablespoons golden raisins

3 tablespoons fresh lemon juice

1 cup fresh bread crumbs, made from French or Italian bread

2 pounds ground beef chuck

2 large eggs

1 medium onion, grated

1 large garlic clove, grated

2 teaspoons salt

Freshly ground pepper

In a large slow cooker, stir together the tomato sauce, ½ cup of the water, the brown sugar, the raisins, and the lemon juice.

Place the bread crumbs in a small bowl with the remaining ½ cup water. Let stand until the water is absorbed. Squeeze the bread and place it in a large bowl.

Add the beef, eggs, onion, garlic, salt, and pepper to taste. Mix well. Moisten your hands in cold water and shape the mixture into 2-inch balls.

Place the meatballs in the slow cooker, spooning some of the sauce over the top. It's OK to make two layers. Cover and cook on low for 5 hours or on high for 2½ hours, or until the meatballs are tender and cooked through. Serve hot.

Meatballs with Feta and Tomato Sauce

GREECE

Cumin and oregano in the meat and a hint of cinnamon in the sauce add a Greek touch to these meatballs. Tuck a few of them into warm pita bread for a great sandwich. They are also good served over cooked rice or orzo pasta.

SERVES 8 TO 10

SAUCE

2   tablespoons olive oil

1   medium onion, chopped

1   28-ounce can crushed tomatoes

½   cup water

½   teaspoon ground cinnamon

   Pinch of crushed red pepper

   Salt

MEATBALLS

2½   pounds ground beef chuck

2   large eggs, beaten

1   medium onion, minced

2   garlic cloves, minced

½   cup plain dry bread crumbs

½   cup finely chopped fresh mint or flat-leaf parsley

2   teaspoons Spanish smoked paprika (see page 20)

1   teaspoon ground cumin

½   teaspoon dried oregano

2   teaspoons salt

½   teaspoon freshly ground pepper

½   cup crumbled feta

2   scallions, thinly sliced

MAKE THE SAUCE: In a large skillet, heat the oil over medium heat. Add the onion and cook, stirring often, until tender and golden, about 10 minutes. Scrape the onion into a large slow cooker. Add the tomatoes, water, cinnamon, crushed red pepper, and salt to taste. Stir well.

MAKE THE MEATBALLS: In a large bowl, combine the meat, eggs, onion, garlic, bread crumbs, mint, paprika, cumin, oregano, salt, and pepper. Mix well. Moisten your hands in cold water and roll the mixture into 2-inch balls.

Place the meatballs in the cooker, spooning some of the sauce over them. It's OK to make more than one layer. Cover and cook on low for 5 to 6 hours, or until cooked through.

Sprinkle the meatballs with the feta and scallions and serve hot.

Spicy Meatball Tagine with Poached Eggs

MOROCCO

These little meatballs cooked in a spicy tomato sauce and topped with poached eggs are irresistible. Middle Eastern spices add an exotic touch. Serve over whole wheat couscous with a big green salad on the side.

SERVES 6

SAUCE

- 1   28-ounce can crushed tomatoes
- ½   cup water
- 1   large onion, finely chopped
- 1   tablespoon Spanish smoked paprika (see page 20)
- 1   tablespoon ground cumin
- Salt
- Pinch of cayenne pepper

MEATBALLS

- 2   pounds ground beef chuck or lamb
- 1   medium onion, grated or finely chopped
- 1   garlic clove, minced
- 1   large egg, beaten
- 1   tablespoon paprika
- 2   teaspoons ground cumin
- ¼   teaspoon cayenne pepper

- 6   large eggs (optional)
- ½   cup chopped fresh cilantro

MAKE THE SAUCE: In a large slow cooker, combine the tomatoes, water, onion, paprika, cumin, salt to taste, and cayenne. Stir well. Cover and cook on low for 4 hours.

MAKE THE MEATBALLS: Combine all the ingredients. Moisten your hands in cold water and shape the mixture into 1-inch balls.

After the sauce has cooked for 4 hours, turn the slow cooker to high. Uncover the pot and drop the meatballs into the simmering sauce. Re-cover and cook for 2 hours more, or until the meatballs are cooked through.

MAKE THE POACHED EGGS, IF USING: When the meatballs are ready, break one of the eggs into a cup. Carefully slip the egg onto the surface of the simmering sauce. Repeat with the remaining 5 eggs. Cover and cook for 10 to 15 minutes, or until the eggs are done to taste.

Serve hot, sprinkled with the cilantro.

Osso Buco

ITALY

Sliced veal shanks, known as *osso buco* in Italy, are cooked with anchovies and finished with gremolata, a sprinkling of freshly chopped garlic, parsley, and lemon zest. The anchovies melt and disappear into the savory sauce, leaving a subtle, elusive flavor.

If the butcher hasn't done so, tie a piece of cooking twine around the outside surface of each shank like a belt. This will help the meat to hold its shape as it cooks. Watch the cooking time on the shanks. If they overcook they can fall apart and won't look as glamorous. Other cuts of veal, such as shoulder chops, can be substituted for the shanks. The taste will be the same.

You can prepare this a day or two ahead of time, but for the best flavor, add the gremolata just before serving. Serve with risotto or, for something different, a puree of celeriac (celery root).

SERVES 6

- ¼ cup olive oil
- 6 cross-cut veal shanks (about 12 ounces each)
- Salt and freshly ground pepper
- 2 medium onions, chopped
- 2 medium carrots, peeled and chopped
- 2 celery ribs, chopped
- 1 2-ounce can anchovy fillets, drained and chopped
- 1 tablespoon plus 1 teaspoon finely chopped garlic
- 1 cup dry white wine
- 1 cup chicken broth
- 2 tablespoons chopped fresh flat-leaf parsley
- 1 teaspoon grated lemon zest

In a large, heavy skillet, heat the oil over medium-high heat. Pat the veal shanks dry with paper towels. Brown the shanks well on all sides, in batches if necessary, about 20 minutes per batch. Place the shanks in a large slow cooker and sprinkle with salt and pepper to taste.

Add the onions, carrots, and celery to the skillet and cook over medium heat, stirring often, until the vegetables are softened, about 10 minutes. Push the vegetables to the side and stir in the anchovies and 1 tablespoon of the garlic. Cook for 2 minutes more, or until the anchovies dissolve. Stir in the wine and chicken broth and bring to a simmer. Scrape the contents of the skillet into the slow cooker.

Cover and cook on low for 5 to 6 hours, or until the meat is very tender and coming away from the bone.

Remove the shanks from the slow cooker and place them on a platter. Cover and keep warm. Skim the fat from the surface of the sauce. Pour the sauce into a small saucepan and bring it to a simmer over high heat. Cook for several minutes, until slightly reduced. Stir in the remaining 1 teaspoon garlic, the parsley, and the lemon zest. Spoon the sauce over the veal shanks and serve hot.

Pork and Lamb

Pork and Lamb

Pork and Pepper Stew with Fennel

ITALY

Pork so tender you can cut it with a spoon is the star of this savory southern Italian–style stew. The dish is also good made with beef or lamb, though you may need to adjust the cooking time. I like to serve it with polenta.

SERVES 6

- ¼ cup olive oil
- 3 pounds boneless pork shoulder, trimmed and cut into 2-inch cubes
  Salt and freshly ground pepper
- 1 large onion, chopped
- 2 garlic cloves
- 1 teaspoon fennel seeds
  Pinch of crushed red pepper
- ½ cup dry white wine
- 1 28-ounce can crushed tomatoes
- ½ cup water
- 2 large red bell peppers, chopped

In a large, heavy skillet, heat the oil over medium-high heat. Pat the pork dry with paper towels and brown it well on all sides, about 20 minutes total. Transfer the pork to a large slow cooker and sprinkle it with salt and pepper to taste.

Add the onion to the skillet and cook, stirring often, until golden and tender, about 10 minutes. Stir in the garlic, fennel, and crushed red pepper. Add the wine, tomatoes, and water, and bring the mixture to a simmer. Scrape the sauce into the slow cooker. Add the peppers.

Cover and cook on low for 6 to 8 hours, or until the meat is very tender and falling apart. Taste for seasonings and serve.

Portuguese Pulled Pork

PORTUGAL

Portuguese fishermen who settled in New Bedford, Massachusetts, brought with them a love for this flavorful pork dish. The traditional way to make it is in a clay pot called a *caçoila*, but a slow cooker is the perfect substitute. The shredded pork is a favorite at street fairs and in local sandwich shops.

Serve it over rice or piled into crisp rolls bathed with the cooking juices and topped with hot pickled peppers. It's great for a casual party.

SERVES 8

- 2 tablespoons olive oil
- 3 pounds boneless pork shoulder, rolled and tied
- Salt and freshly ground pepper
- 2 large onions, sliced
- 4 garlic cloves, finely chopped
- ¼ cup red wine vinegar
- ¼ teaspoon crushed red pepper
- 2 tablespoons Spanish smoked paprika (see page 20)
- ¼ teaspoon ground cinnamon
- 1 cup water

In a large, heavy skillet, heat the oil over medium-high heat. Pat the pork dry with paper towels and brown it well on all sides, about 20 minutes total. Transfer the pork to a large slow cooker and sprinkle with salt and pepper to taste.

Add the onions and garlic to the skillet and cook, stirring often, until the onions are tender and golden, about 10 minutes. Stir in the vinegar and bring to a simmer. Pour the mixture over the pork. Add the crushed red pepper, paprika, cinnamon, water, and salt and pepper to taste. Cover and cook on low for 8 to 10 hours, or until the meat is fork-tender.

Transfer the meat to a cutting board, but leave the sauce in the slow cooker with the heat on. With two forks, tear the meat into bite-size pieces. Return the meat to the slow cooker to reheat, then serve.

Pork Ragu with Broken Lasagna Maialino Style

ITALY

Maialino restaurant in New York City serves this hearty pork ragu as a sauce for dried lasagna pasta that has been broken into 3-inch pieces. The dish is unusual in that it has no tomatoes—just onion, celery, and fennel seeds for flavor. At the end of the cooking, the meat is torn into small pieces and tossed with the cooked pasta, grated cheese, and fresh arugula for a little color and texture. I adapted this recipe from one that appeared in the *New York Times*.

This makes a lot of sauce. If you don't want to use it all at once, pack some of it away in the freezer for another meal. It's also good with polenta or cooked beans instead of pasta.

SERVES 6 TO 8; MAKES 12 CUPS MEAT AND SAUCE

SAUCE

4 pounds bone-in pork shoulder

Salt and freshly ground pepper

3 tablespoons olive oil

1 medium white onion, cut into large pieces

1 celery rib, cut into large pieces

1 teaspoon fennel seeds

4 cups Chicken Broth (page 44) or store-bought chicken broth

3 fresh thyme sprigs

PASTA

Salt

1 pound dried pasta, such as broken lasagna

2 tablespoons unsalted butter

¼ cup freshly grated Parmigiano-Reggiano

2 cups trimmed baby arugula

MAKE THE SAUCE: Using a sharp knife, remove the thick skin from the pork, leaving a small amount of fat on top of the meat. Season with salt and pepper to taste. Place the pork in a large slow cooker.

In a large skillet, heat the oil over medium heat. Add the onion, celery, and fennel seeds and cook, stirring often, until the vegetables are softened, about 10 minutes. Add the broth and thyme and bring to a simmer.

Add the contents of the skillet to the slow cooker. The meat should be almost covered by the liquid. If not, add some water. Cover and cook on low for 8 to 10 hours, until the meat just begins to pull away from the bone and a small sharp knife inserted in the meat comes out easily.

Place the meat on a cutting board. With two forks, tear the meat into bite-size pieces and discard the bones. Place the meat in a bowl.

Strain the cooking liquid into another bowl. Skim off the excess fat. Discard the solids. Pour enough of the cooking liquid over the pork to cover it. (Save the remainder to use for soup or stews.) When ready to serve, reheat the pork in its liquid in a large pot. Simmer until the liquid is slightly reduced.

MAKE THE PASTA: Meanwhile, bring a large pot of salted water to a boil over high heat. Add the pasta and cook, stirring often, until the pasta is tender yet firm to the bite. Drain well.

Add the pasta to the pot with the meat. Add the butter and Parmesan and stir well. Stir in the arugula. Serve immediately.

Pork Ribs with Tomato Balsamic Sauce

ITALY

Balsamic vinegar adds a sweet, tangy flavor to this fennel-accented sauce. I like to use meaty country-style pork ribs.

SERVES 6

- 2 tablespoons olive oil
- 4 pounds country-style bone-in pork ribs
  Salt and freshly ground pepper
- 2 medium carrots, peeled and chopped
- 1 medium onion, chopped
- 4 garlic cloves, finely chopped
- 1 teaspoon fennel seeds
- ½ teaspoon crushed red pepper
- 1 cup dry white wine
- 2 tablespoons balsamic vinegar
- 1 28-ounce can crushed tomatoes
  Chopped fresh flat-leaf parsley

In a large, heavy skillet, heat the oil over medium-high heat. Pat the pork ribs dry with paper towels. Add the ribs to the skillet, in batches if necessary, and cook until they are nicely browned on all sides, about 15 minutes per batch. Transfer the ribs to a large slow cooker and sprinkle with salt and pepper to taste.

Discard all but 2 tablespoons of fat from the skillet. Add the carrots and onion. Cook, stirring occasionally, until softened, about 10 minutes. Add the garlic, fennel seeds, and crushed red pepper and stir well. Add the wine and vinegar and bring to a simmer. Stir in the tomatoes. Add 1 teaspoon salt and pour the mixture over the ribs in the slow cooker.

Cover and cook on low for 6 hours, or until the meat is tender and coming away from the bones.

Skim the fat from the surface of the sauce. Taste for seasonings. Serve hot, sprinkled with parsley.

Pork Ribs with Smoked Paprika Sauce

If you think paprika means tasteless red dust, you haven't tried genuine Spanish paprika. It comes in several varieties, from sweet to hot. The flavor is smoky, since it is made from small red peppers dried over a fire.

In this recipe, pork ribs cook in a distinctive sauce flavored with Spanish paprika and sherry vinegar. The color is a deep rich red, and the flavor is tangy and unique. Serve these ribs with cooked beans or chickpeas and a hearty green vegetable such as kale.

SERVES 6

> 2 tablespoons olive oil
>
> 4 pounds meaty bone-in pork ribs, cut into individual ribs
>   Salt and freshly ground pepper
>
> 2 medium onions, sliced
>
> 3 large garlic cloves, chopped
>
> 2 cups beef broth, Chicken Broth (page 44),
>   or store-bought chicken broth
>
> 2 tablespoons sherry vinegar or red wine vinegar
>
> 2 tablespoons Spanish smoked paprika (see page 20)

In a large, heavy skillet, heat the oil over medium heat. Pat the ribs dry with paper towels. Add as many of the ribs to the skillet as will fit comfortably without crowding. Brown the ribs on all sides, about 15 minutes per batch. Place the browned ribs in a large slow cooker and sprinkle with salt and pepper to taste.

Pour off all but 1 tablespoon of the fat from the skillet. Add the onions and cook, stirring often, for 10 minutes, or until tender. Stir in the garlic and cook for 1 minute. Stir in the broth, vinegar, and paprika, scraping the bottom of the pan. Bring to a simmer and cook for 1 minute. Pour the liquid over the ribs in the slow cooker. Stir to coat the ribs.

Cover and cook on low for 6 to 8 hours, or until the meat is coming away from the bones.

Remove the ribs from the sauce. Skim the fat from the surface of the sauce. Taste for seasonings. Pour the sauce over the ribs and serve hot.

Pork and White Bean Casserole

SPAIN

Known as *fabada*, this bean casserole is from the Asturias region of Spain. It is usually made with a special type of large white bean called *fabes*, but dried lima beans are a good substitute, or you can use another white bean, such as Great Northern. *Morcilla* is a blood sausage that is popular in Spain, but I've made this with fully cooked Spanish chorizo, which is readily available.

Like many stewed and braised dishes, this is even more flavorful after an overnight rest and reheating. If you like, make it ahead to enjoy later in the week after a busy day. Serve it with a green salad dressed with oil and vinegar.

SERVES 8

- 1 pound dried Spanish fabes (see headnote), large lima beans, or other white beans, rinsed, drained, and picked over
- 6 garlic cloves, finely chopped
- 1 medium onion, peeled but left whole
- 1 bay leaf
- 1 teaspoon Spanish smoked paprika (see page 20) or regular paprika
- 1 smoked ham hock (about 12 ounces)
- 1 pound Spanish morcilla (see headnote) or fully cooked chorizo sausage
- 6 cups water
- Salt

Place the beans in a large bowl. Add water to cover by 1 inch. Let stand for several hours or overnight.

Drain the beans and place them in a large slow cooker with the garlic, onion, bay leaf, paprika, ham hock, sausage, water, and salt to taste. Cover and cook on low for 8 to 10 hours, or until the beans are very tender. Taste for seasoning.

Remove and discard the bay leaf and the onion. Remove the ham hock, discarding the skin and bones. Cut the meat into bite-size pieces. Slice the sausage. Return the ham and sausage to the pot with the beans. Serve hot.

Pork and Lamb Ragu

ITALY

This rich ragu gets its flavor from chunks of pork and lamb. The meat is on the bone, so it has an extra depth of flavor. The vegetables are removed at the end of the cooking time, leaving behind just a hint of their sweet flavor. This makes enough sauce to feed a crowd, or you can divide it into containers to freeze for future meals. It's good on pasta, rice, or polenta.

SERVES 8; MAKES 10 CUPS MEAT AND SAUCE

- 2 tablespoons olive oil
- 2½ pounds bone-in pork ribs or shoulder
- 1½ pounds boneless lamb shoulder, cut into 2-inch chunks
-   Salt and freshly ground pepper
- 1 cup dry red wine
- 2 28-ounce cans crushed tomatoes
- 1 cup water
- 2 medium onions, peeled but left whole
- 2 celery ribs, trimmed and left whole
- 2 medium carrots, peeled and left whole

In a large, heavy skillet, heat the oil over medium-high heat. Pat the meat dry with paper towels. Add as much meat to the skillet as will fit comfortably without crowding. Cook, turning the meat occasionally, until nicely browned on all sides, about 15 minutes per batch. Place the browned meat in a large slow cooker. Sprinkle with salt and pepper to taste.

Pour off the excess fat from the skillet. Add the wine and bring it to a simmer, scraping the bottom of the pan. Cook for 1 minute.

Add the contents of the skillet, the tomatoes, water, and vegetables to the slow cooker. Add 1 teaspoon salt and pepper to taste. Cover and cook on low for 8 hours, or until the meat is coming away from the bone.

Discard the vegetables and any loose bones. Remove the meat and skim the fat from the surface of the sauce. Taste for seasonings.

Pour the sauce over the meat and serve hot.

Lamb and Pine Nut Meatballs

MIDDLE EAST

Pine nuts and sweet spices make these lamb meatballs unusually flavorful. Instead of chopping the onion, try grating it on a Microplane or box grater for a fine texture that infuses the meat. A grater works well with garlic cloves too, but watch your fingertips!

These tasty meatballs are good on couscous or rice, but my favorite way to serve them is stuffed into pita bread and topped with a dollop of creamy Greek yogurt or Tzatziki (page 72) and chopped cilantro.

SERVES 6 TO 8

- 4 garlic cloves, grated or minced
- 1 28-ounce can crushed tomatoes
- 2 cups water
- 2 tablespoons fresh lemon juice
- Pinch of cayenne pepper
- Salt
- 2 slices day-old French bread
- 2 pounds ground lamb
- 2 large eggs, beaten
- 1 medium onion, grated
- ½ cup pine nuts, toasted
- ¼ cup chopped fresh flat-leaf parsley
- 1 teaspoon grated lemon zest
- ½ teaspoon ground cumin
- ½ teaspoon ground cinnamon
- ¼ teaspoon ground allspice
- Freshly ground pepper
- Chopped fresh cilantro

Set aside 1 teaspoon of the garlic for the meatball mixture. In a medium bowl, stir together the remaining garlic, tomatoes, 1 cup water, lemon juice, cayenne, and 1 teaspoon salt. Pour half of the sauce into a large slow cooker.

Tear the bread into small pieces and place in a small bowl. Add the remaining 1 cup water and let stand for 15 minutes. Drain off the water and squeeze the bread to remove the excess liquid. Crumble the bread very fine and place it in a large bowl.

Add the reserved 1 teaspoon garlic, the lamb, eggs, onion, pine nuts, parsley, lemon zest, cumin, cinnamon, allspice, 1½ teaspoons salt, and pepper to taste. Moisten your hands in cold water and shape the mixture into 2-inch balls.

Place the meatballs in the slow cooker. It's OK to make two layers. Pour on the remaining sauce. Cover and cook on low for 5 hours, or until the meatballs are tender and cooked through.

Serve hot, sprinkled with cilantro.

Turkish Lamb Meat Loaf

TURKEY

I'm lucky enough to live in an area with several very good Turkish restaurants. Whenever I eat at one of them, I can't resist the grilled kebabs called *köfte*, which are made from ground lamb seasoned with onions and spices and served with tomato sauce, rice, and grilled vegetables.

This is my version, turned into a tasty slow-cooker meat loaf. If you prefer, substitute ground beef or turkey for the lamb. The dish is great hot or cold.

SERVES 8

- 2 pounds ground lamb
- 1 large egg, lightly beaten
- 1 large red bell pepper, finely chopped
- 1 medium onion, grated
- 3 garlic cloves, finely chopped
- ½ cup chopped fresh flat-leaf parsley
- ½ cup plain dry bread crumbs
- 1 tablespoon ground cumin
- Salt and freshly ground pepper
- All-Purpose Tomato Sauce (page 199; optional)

Fold a 2-foot length of aluminum foil in half lengthwise. Place the foil into the insert of a large slow cooker, pressing it against the bottom and up the sides. Spray the foil and the insert with nonstick cooking spray.

In a large bowl, combine the lamb, egg, bell pepper, onion, garlic, parsley, bread crumbs, cumin, and salt and pepper to taste. Mix well. Moisten your hands in cold water and shape the mixture into a loaf slightly smaller than the insert of the cooker. Carefully place the loaf into the cooker on top of the foil. Cover and cook on high for 3 to 3½ hours, or until an instant-read thermometer inserted in the center of the loaf registers 165°F to 170°F.

Carefully lift the meat loaf out of the slow cooker, using the ends of the foil as handles. Slide the meat loaf onto a serving platter. Cut into slices and serve hot, with the tomato sauce, if using.

Bandits' Lamb

GREECE

According to an old Greek tale, bandits would sneak down from their mountain hideaway to steal food from the farmers. Once back in their lair, the clever thieves devised a unique way to cook the meat so that the smoke and smell of the cooking would not reveal their location. They dug a hole in the ground, partially filled it with hot coals, placed the purloined food into the hole, and covered it. Since nothing escaped the pot, the seasonings infused the meat and vegetables during the long, slow cooking and gave the dish heavenly flavor.

Any lamb seasoned this way cooks perfectly in the slow cooker—no digging required! The sharp cheese, garlic, and fresh rosemary become mellow, imparting a pronounced, aromatic flavor to the lamb and potatoes.

SERVES 8

- 4 pounds boneless leg of lamb
- 2 tablespoons olive oil, plus more for the insert
  Salt and freshly ground pepper
- 6 garlic cloves, finely chopped
- 2 tablespoons chopped fresh rosemary
- 2 ounces sharp sheep's milk cheese, such as Greek Kefalotyri or Pecorino Romano, cut into thin slices
- 2 pounds boiling potatoes, such as Yukon Gold or red, cut into thick slices
- 4 medium carrots, peeled and cut into thick slices
- ½ cup beef or chicken broth

Place the meat on a cutting board boned side up. Rub it with the 2 tablespoons olive oil and sprinkle with salt and pepper to taste. Reserve half of the garlic and rosemary and sprinkle the lamb with the remainder. Top with the cheese slices. Carefully roll up the meat, tucking in the cheese slices to make a compact roast. Tie the roast crosswise in several places with kitchen twine.

Oil the insert of a large slow cooker. Place the potatoes, carrots, and broth in the cooker. Sprinkle with the remaining rosemary and garlic and salt and pepper to taste. Toss to combine. Place the lamb on top of the vegetables. Cover and cook on low for 6 to 8 hours, or until the meat is tender when pierced with a knife.

Remove the meat to a cutting board. With a slotted spoon, transfer the vegetables to a serving platter. Cover and keep warm.

Slice the meat and arrange it over the vegetables. Skim the fat from the surface of the sauce. Taste for seasonings. Pour the sauce over the meat and vegetables and serve hot.

Provençal Lamb Pot Roast

FRANCE

It doesn't get much simpler than this classic pot roast. Just put the lamb, tomatoes, and seasonings into the cooker, turn it on, and come back 8 hours later to a meal of tender lamb in a garlicky tomato sauce. Serve it with wide egg noodles, steamed broccoli, and a bottle of Cabernet Sauvignon for a memorable meal.

SERVES 6 TO 8

- 4 pounds boneless lamb shoulder, rolled and tied
- 1 28-ounce can tomatoes, drained and chopped
  Salt and freshly ground pepper
- 1 tablespoon chopped fresh rosemary or ½ teaspoon crumbled dried
- 1 3-inch strip orange zest
- 12 whole garlic cloves, peeled

Place the lamb in a large slow cooker. Pour the tomatoes over the lamb. Sprinkle with 1 teaspoon salt, 1 teaspoon pepper, and the rosemary. Add the orange zest and scatter the garlic cloves around the lamb.

Cover and cook on low for 8 to 10 hours, or until the meat is tender when pierced with a fork. Remove the lamb from the cooker. Cover and keep warm.

Skim the fat from the surface of the sauce. Remove the orange zest and smash the garlic into the sauce with the back of a spoon. Taste for seasonings.

Carve the lamb and serve it hot, with the sauce.

Lamb Shanks with Sweet and Sour Onions

ITALY

Red onions have a sweet flavor that is complemented here by red wine and balsamic vinegar. Serve with buttery golden polenta or mashed potatoes with Parmigiano-Reggiano.

While I prefer serving smaller, individual shanks, they can be hard to find. In that case, I buy only 4 or 5 larger shanks and carve the meat from the bone before serving.

SERVES 6

- 6 small or 4 large lamb shanks, well trimmed
- Salt and freshly ground pepper
- 2 tablespoons olive oil
- 2 pounds red onions (about 5 medium), sliced
- 4 garlic cloves, finely chopped
- 1 tablespoon chopped fresh rosemary
- 1 cup dry red wine
- ¼ cup balsamic vinegar

Sprinkle the shanks with salt and pepper. Place them in a large slow cooker.

In a medium skillet, heat the oil over medium heat. Add the onions and cook, stirring often, until tender and just beginning to brown, about 12 minutes. Add the garlic and rosemary and cook for 1 minute more. Stir in the wine, vinegar, and salt and pepper to taste. Bring the liquid to a simmer and cook for 1 minute. Pour the mixture over the lamb.

Cover and cook on low for 6 to 8 hours, or until the meat is tender and coming away from the bone. Transfer the shanks to a serving platter. Cover and keep warm.

Skim the fat from the surface of the sauce. Taste for seasonings. Carve the meat from the bones if you used large shanks. Pour the onions and sauce over the meat and serve hot.

Braised Lamb Shanks with Red Wine and Spices

GREECE

Low heat coaxes out the flavor of the lamb shanks and melts away any tough tendons. A cinnamon stick, anchovies, and juniper berries add depth to the sauce. The anchovies contribute savoriness, then disappear. Juniper berries can be found in supermarkets with large spice departments.

SERVES 6

- 3 tablespoons olive oil
- 6 small or 4 large lamb shanks, well trimmed
  Salt and freshly ground pepper
- 2 medium onions, chopped
- 2 celery ribs, chopped
- 2 medium carrots, peeled and chopped
- 4 garlic cloves, finely chopped
- 6 canned anchovy fillets, drained and chopped
- 2 tablespoons tomato paste
- 4 juniper berries
- 1 cinnamon stick
- 1 bay leaf
- 1 cup dry red wine
- 2 cups Chicken Broth (page 44) or store-bought broth

In a large, heavy skillet, heat the oil over medium-high heat. Pat the shanks dry with paper towels and brown them on all sides, in batches if necessary, about 15 minutes per batch. Place the browned shanks in a large slow cooker and sprinkle with salt and pepper to taste.

Add the onions, celery, and carrots to the skillet. Cook, stirring often, over medium heat, until the vegetables are tender and golden, about 10 minutes. Stir in the garlic, anchovies, and tomato paste and cook for 1 minute more. Stir in the juniper berries, cinnamon stick, bay leaf, and wine and bring to a simmer.

Pour the sauce over the lamb shanks. Add the broth. Cover and cook on low for 6 to 8 hours, or until the meat is tender and coming away from the bone.

Transfer the shanks to a serving platter. Cover and keep warm. Skim the fat from the surface of the sauce. Remove and discard the bay leaf, cinnamon stick, and juniper berries. Carve the meat from the bones if you used large shanks, spoon the sauce over the meat, and serve hot.

Pasta, Grains, and Beans

Pasta, Grains, and Beans

Pasta with Spicy Cauliflower and Anchovy Crumbs

ITALY

Sicilian cooks have a knack for making something delicious out of the simplest of ingredients. Nothing goes to waste, not even bread that is no longer fresh. Toasted with olive oil and anchovies, bread crumbs make a tasty, crunchy topping to sprinkle on pasta in a tomato and cauliflower sauce.

SERVES 6

- 1 28-ounce can crushed tomatoes
- 1 cup water
- 5 tablespoons olive oil
- 2 garlic cloves, finely chopped
- ½ teaspoon dried oregano
- Salt
- Pinch of crushed red pepper
- 1 small cauliflower, trimmed and cut into ½-inch pieces
- 4 canned anchovy fillets, drained
- ⅓ cup plain dry bread crumbs
- Freshly ground pepper
- 1 pound fusilli or other dried pasta, cooked and drained

In a large slow cooker, stir together the tomatoes, water, 2 tablespoons of the oil, the garlic, oregano, 1 teaspoon salt, and the crushed red pepper. Add the cauliflower. Cover and cook on high for 3 hours, or until the cauliflower is very tender.

Meanwhile, heat the remaining 3 tablespoons oil in a small skillet. Add the anchovies and cook over medium heat, stirring constantly, until they are almost dissolved, about 3 minutes. Add the bread crumbs and cook, stirring often, until they are toasty, about 5 minutes more. Season with black pepper to taste.

Toss the cauliflower sauce with the pasta. Top with the anchovy crumbs. Serve immediately.

Polenta with Herbs

ITALY

Made the traditional way on the stovetop, polenta has to be stirred constantly, but this slow cooker method leaves you free. It's an ideal side dish to serve with all kinds of vegetable and meat stews. Try it with other herb and cheese combinations too, such as goat cheese and thyme or basil and feta.

SERVES 6

- 3 cups water
- 2 cups Chicken Broth (page 44), Vegetable Broth (page 45), or store-bought broth
- 1 cup coarsely ground yellow cornmeal, preferably stone-ground
- 1 teaspoon salt
- ¼ cup extra-virgin olive oil
- 1 tablespoon chopped fresh rosemary
- ½ cup freshly grated Parmigiano-Reggiano
  Freshly ground pepper

In a large slow cooker, stir together the water, broth, cornmeal, and salt. Cover and cook on high for 2 hours. Stir well, cover, and cook for 30 to 60 minutes more, or until the polenta is thick.

Turn off the heat. Stir in the olive oil, rosemary, Parmesan, and pepper to taste. Serve hot.

Truffled Polenta

ITALY

Truffles are tubers that grow on the roots of certain trees. Because they are scarce, they are quite expensive. But reasonably priced truffle butter has recently become widely available, and I like to use it to add a luxurious touch to all kinds of foods, from fresh pasta to steamed vegetables and rice pilaf. Here, it contributes great flavor to rich, creamy polenta, making this recipe ideal for a sophisticated dinner party.

SERVES 8

- 3 cups water
- 2 cups whole milk
- 1 cup coarsely ground yellow cornmeal, preferably stone-ground
  Salt
- 2 tablespoons white truffle butter, or to taste
- 2 tablespoons unsalted butter

In a large slow cooker, stir together the water, milk, cornmeal, and 1 teaspoon salt. Cover and cook on high for 2 hours. Stir well, cover, and cook for 30 to 60 minutes more, or until the polenta is thick.

Turn off the heat. Stir in the truffle butter and unsalted butter. Taste for seasonings. Serve hot.

Polenta with Spinach and Ricotta

ITALY

This creamy combination of cornmeal with spinach and cheese makes a fine meatless meal, or it can be served as a side dish with meat or fish.

Good ricotta should be creamy and sweet tasting. Avoid brands that have an off-white color or a gritty texture.

SERVES 8

- 5 cups water
- 1 cup coarsely ground yellow cornmeal, preferably stone-ground
  Salt
- 1 10-ounce package frozen chopped spinach, thawed and drained
- 1 cup whole-milk ricotta
- 2 tablespoons unsalted butter
  Freshly ground pepper
- ¾ cup freshly grated Parmigiano-Reggiano

In a large slow cooker, stir together the water, cornmeal, and 1 teaspoon salt. Cover and cook on high for 2 hours. Stir well, cover, and cook for 30 to 60 minutes more, or until the polenta is thick.

Stir in the spinach, ricotta, butter, and pepper to taste, and cook for 10 minutes more. Stir in the Parmesan. Taste for seasonings. Serve hot.

Polenta Lasagna

ITALY

Layers of golden polenta take the place of pasta in this cheesy "lasagna." Slices of time-saving prepared polenta are smothered with cheese, spinach, mushrooms, and tomato sauce, then slow cooked for a colorful take on a familiar recipe.

Packaged in plastic tubes like cookie dough, store-bought polenta is firm, so it slices beautifully. It is good baked, grilled, or fried in a bit of butter or oil. You can find it in most supermarkets.

SERVES 8

- 8 ounces sweet Italian pork or turkey sausages
- 1 10-ounce box frozen chopped spinach, thawed
- 2 tablespoons olive oil, plus more for the insert
- 1 8- to 10-ounce package white mushrooms, sliced
  Salt and freshly ground pepper
- 3 cups All-Purpose Tomato Sauce (page 199)
- 2 1-pound tubes prepared polenta, thinly sliced
- 8 ounces mozzarella, diced
- 1 cup freshly grated Parmigiano-Reggiano

Place the sausages in a small skillet. Add water to a depth of ½ inch. Cover and cook over medium heat until the water is evaporated and the sausages begin to brown, about 10 minutes. Uncover and cook, turning the sausages occasionally, until cooked through, 5 to 10 minutes more. Transfer the sausages to a plate. Let cool slightly, then cut the sausages into thin slices.

Place the spinach in a towel and squeeze to extract as much of the liquid as possible.

Heat the 2 tablespoons olive oil in a medium skillet. Add the mushrooms and salt and pepper to taste. Cook, stirring occasionally, until the juices evaporate and the mushrooms are browned, about 10 minutes.

Oil the insert of a large slow cooker. Spoon 1 cup of the sauce into the cooker. Make a layer of about one third of the polenta slices, overlapping them slightly. Sprinkle with one half of the sausage slices, spinach, mozzarella, and mushrooms. Sprinkle with one third of the Parmesan. Make a second layer of half of the remaining polenta, 1 cup of the sauce, and the remaining sausage, spinach, mozzarella, and mushrooms. Sprinkle with half of the remaining Parmesan. Top with the remaining polenta, sauce, and Parmesan.

Cover and cook on high for 4 hours, or until the sauce is bubbling around the edges and the center is hot.

Uncover and let stand for 15 minutes before serving. Run a knife around the edge of the insert, cut the lasagna into wedges, and serve hot.

Wheat Berry Tabbouleh

LEBANON/MIDDLE EAST

In Lebanon and throughout the Middle East, bulgur, which is cracked wheat that has been partially cooked, is used to make tabbouleh, but this refreshing salad is even better when made with whole unprocessed wheat berries. I like their dense, chewy texture and nutty flavor.

Wheat berries can be cooked on the stovetop, but I prefer to use the slow cooker, since I don't have to worry about their boiling over or scorching. There are several forms of wheat berries on the market, so be prepared to adjust the cooking time according to the variety you find. The best way to tell whether they are done is to taste them. They should be tender yet still firm, with no raw starch flavor.

Serve the salad with feta cheese and warm pita bread for lunch or as a side dish with a sandwich, grilled chicken, or fish.

SERVES 8

- 2 cups wheat berries, rinsed and drained
- 4 cups water
- Salt
- ¼ cup olive oil
- 2–3 tablespoons fresh lemon juice
- Freshly ground pepper
- About 3 cups chopped fresh flat-leaf parsley (from 2 or 3 bunches)
- 1 cup chopped fresh mint
- 6 scallions, finely chopped
- 2 medium tomatoes
- 2 medium Kirby cucumbers, trimmed and chopped
- Romaine lettuce leaves

Place the wheat berries in a large slow cooker. Add the water and 1 teaspoon salt.

Cover and cook on high for 2 hours, or until the wheat berries are tender but still chewy.

Drain the wheat berries if necessary. Transfer to a large bowl. Let the wheat berries cool to lukewarm, stirring occasionally.

In a small bowl, whisk together the oil, 2 tablespoons of the lemon juice, and salt and pepper to taste. Add the dressing to the wheat berries and toss well. Stir in the chopped herbs and scallions. Cut the tomatoes in half and squeeze them to extract the seeds. Chop the tomatoes and add them to the bowl along with the cucumbers. Taste for seasonings and add the remaining tablespoon lemon juice if desired. Spoon the salad onto the lettuce leaves and serve at room temperature.

Bulgur and Toasted Walnut Pilaf

MIDDLE EAST

Parboiled wheat that has been dried and crushed, bulgur comes in several sizes, from fine to coarse. When cooked, it has a warm nutty flavor and slightly chewy texture. In this recipe, bulgur is mixed with vegetables and toasted walnuts to make a pilaf. It is a nice alternative to rice.

SERVES 6 TO 8

- 2 cups coarse bulgur
- 5 cups Chicken Broth (page 44) or Vegetable Broth (page 45), or store-bought broth
- 6 scallions, finely chopped
- 1 medium red or yellow bell pepper, chopped
- 1 medium zucchini, chopped
- Salt and freshly ground pepper
- ½ cup walnuts, toasted and coarsely chopped

In a large slow cooker, combine the bulgur, broth, scallions, bell pepper, zucchini, 1 teaspoon salt, and pepper to taste. Stir well.

Cover and cook on high for 1½ to 2 hours or on low for 3 to 4 hours, or until the bulgur is tender yet still chewy. Toss well and serve hot, sprinkled with the walnuts.

Vegetable Bulgur Pilaf

TURKEY

Peppers, tomatoes, spinach, and onions add great flavor to this bulgur pilaf. The best peppers to use are mild long green peppers such as Anaheim or Italian frying peppers, but bell peppers are good too. The fresh spinach is added at the end of the cooking time so that it just wilts from the heat of the pilaf. I like to serve this with grilled lamb chops or kebabs.

SERVES 8 TO 10

3 tablespoons unsweetened butter

2 medium onions, finely chopped

2 mild long green peppers, such as Anaheim, chopped

Salt and freshly ground pepper

2 cups coarse bulgur

2 medium tomatoes, chopped

1 teaspoon Spanish smoked paprika (see page 20)

5 cups Chicken Broth (page 44), Vegetable Broth (page 45), or store-bought broth

8 ounces spinach, tough stems removed, chopped

Melt 2 tablespoons of the butter in a large, heavy skillet over medium heat. Add the onions and cook, stirring occasionally, until the onions are tender and golden, about 10 minutes. Stir in the peppers and salt and pepper to taste. Cook for 10 minutes more, or until the peppers are softened.

Scrape the contents of the skillet into a large slow cooker. Add the bulgur, tomatoes, paprika, 1 teaspoon salt, and pepper to taste. Add the broth and stir well.

Cover and cook on high for 1½ to 2 hours or on low for 3 to 4 hours, or until the bulgur is tender yet still chewy.

Stir in the remaining 1 tablespoon butter and the spinach. Taste for seasonings and serve hot.

Farro with Spring Vegetables

ITALY

Farro is a grain similar to wheat, with a warm nutty flavor and a chewy texture. In Italy, grains of farro are cooked whole in soup or braised in broth, as in this recipe. If you can't find farro, substitute spelt, wheat berries, or barley, but keep in mind that you may need to adjust the cooking time.

SERVES 6 TO 8

- 4 tablespoons (½ stick) unsalted butter
- 1 medium onion, finely chopped
- 2 cups farro, rinsed
- 4 cups Chicken Broth (page 44), Vegetable Broth (page 45), or store-bought broth
- Salt and freshly ground pepper
- 1 cup frozen peas, thawed
- 1 cup frozen lima beans, thawed
- ½ cup finely chopped scallions
- ¼ cup freshly grated Parmigiano-Reggiano

In a small skillet, melt 2 tablespoons of the butter over medium heat. Add the onion and cook, stirring often, until the onion is tender, about 10 minutes. Scrape the onion into a large slow cooker.

Pick over the farro and discard any black or shriveled pieces. Place the farro, broth, 1 teaspoon salt, and pepper to taste in the cooker and stir well. Cover and cook on high for 1½ hours.

Stir in the peas, lima beans, and scallions. Cover and cook until the farro is tender yet still chewy and the liquid is absorbed, 15 to 30 minutes more.

Stir in the remaining 2 tablespoons butter and the Parmesan. Taste for seasonings. Serve hot.

Basic Chickpeas

One of the most ancient foods known to humans, chickpeas are an essential ingredient in kitchens all over the Mediterranean. Dried chickpeas are extremely hard in texture, so I cook them a little differently than I cook other beans.

They benefit from soaking overnight, and it's essential to cook them at a high temperature. They take several hours, and the time varies according to the type of cooker you are using and the age of the chickpeas. To be sure they are done when you need them, plan to cook them well in advance of serving them. They will keep in the refrigerator for up to 3 days or in the freezer for 3 months, and they reheat beautifully.

MAKES 6 CUPS

- 1 pound dried chickpeas, rinsed, drained, and picked over
- 1 medium onion, peeled but left whole
- 1 bay leaf
  Salt

Place the chickpeas in a large bowl with cold water to cover by several inches. Soak in a cool place for 6 hours or overnight in the refrigerator. Drain the beans. Pick them over and discard any loose skins or shriveled beans.

Place the chickpeas, onion, and bay leaf in a large slow cooker. Add fresh water to cover by 1 inch and 1 tablespoon salt.

Cover and cook on high for 3 to 5 hours, or until the chickpeas are completely tender. Try more than one to be sure. Taste for seasoning. Discard the onion, bay leaf, and any loose skins.

Remove the chickpeas with a slotted spoon and serve hot as a side dish, or store them in their liquid and use them in salads, soups, and stews.

OUT OF THE POT Country Chickpea Salad

GREECE

Once you have cooked chickpeas on hand, it's easy to put together tasty salads like this one, inspired by the classic Greek salad. A few pickled peperoncini (hot Italian peppers from a jar) add a spicy bite, but you can substitute a sweet pickled pepper if you prefer. This is great as a meal or with a salami sandwich.

SERVES 6 TO 8

- ¼ cup extra-virgin olive oil
- 2–3 tablespoons fresh lemon juice
- ½ teaspoon dried oregano
  Salt and freshly ground pepper
- 3 cups Basic Chickpeas (page 175), drained, or two 16-ounce cans chickpeas, drained
- ½ cup chopped red onion
- ½ cup diced peeled cucumber
- ½ small green bell pepper, chopped
- ½ cup pitted Greek black olives
- ½ cup crumbled feta cheese
- 6 pickled peperoncini
- 1 large tomato, cut into wedges

In a small bowl, whisk together the oil, lemon juice to taste, oregano, and salt and pepper to taste. Toss the chickpeas with half of the dressing in a large bowl. Add the onion, cucumber, green pepper, and olives and toss well.

Pile the chickpeas on a serving platter. Drizzle the remaining dressing over them and sprinkle with the cheese. Garnish with the peperoncini and tomato and serve.

OUT OF THE POT Hummus

Delicious and nutritious, homemade hummus is so much better than the packaged kind. Here is a basic recipe. Be sure to try the variations that follow too.

Serve hummus as a spread or dip for warm pita bread, crackers, or raw vegetables.

MAKES 2½ CUPS

3	cups Basic Chickpeas (page 175) or two 16-ounce cans chickpeas
2	garlic cloves, peeled
¼	cup stirred tahini
3	tablespoons extra-virgin olive oil
3–4	tablespoons fresh lemon juice
	Salt
	Ground sumac or Spanish smoked paprika (see page 20; optional)

Drain the chickpeas and reserve the liquid. In a food processor, finely chop the chickpeas and garlic. Add the tahini, 2 tablespoons of the olive oil, 3 tablespoons of the lemon juice, and salt to taste. Process until smooth, adding some of the reserved liquid as needed. Taste for seasonings, adding more lemon juice and salt if needed.

Spread the hummus in a shallow dish. Drizzle with the remaining 1 tablespoon oil and sprinkle with the sumac. Serve lightly chilled or at room temperature.

Variations

• ROASTED RED PEPPER HUMMUS Add 1 cup drained, chopped roasted red peppers (see page 66) and process until smooth.

• HERBED HUMMUS Stir ¼ cup chopped fresh flat-leaf parsley or cilantro into plain or Roasted Red Pepper Hummus.

OUT OF THE POT *Chickpea, Roasted Pepper, and Bacon Salad*

SPAIN

This salad is good at room temperature and lends itself well to a buffet or picnic side dish. Sometimes I serve it on a bed of baby lettuce with hard-cooked eggs or good canned tuna for lunch or as an appetizer salad.

SERVES 4

- ¼ cup extra-virgin olive oil
- 2 teaspoons sherry vinegar or red wine vinegar
- 1 teaspoon Dijon mustard
- 1 small garlic clove, minced
- Salt and freshly ground pepper
- 3 cups Basic Chickpeas (page 175), drained
- 1½ cups thinly sliced roasted red pepper (jarred, drained, or homemade; see page 66)
- 1 small red onion, thinly sliced
- 8 ounces bacon, cooked, drained, and chopped
- 3 tablespoons chopped fresh flat-leaf parsley

In a large bowl, whisk together the oil, vinegar, mustard, garlic, and salt and pepper to taste.

Add the chickpeas, red pepper, and onion and stir well. Taste for seasonings. Just before serving, stir in the bacon and sprinkle with the parsley.

Lentils with Cream and Crispy Bacon

FRANCE

This recipe turns even people who think they don't like lentils into lentil lovers. The combination of tender lentils and creamy garlic and shallot sauce tossed with crispy bacon is rich and irresistible. Perfect for a hearty winter meal with grilled salmon or chops.

SERVES 8

- 1 pound lentils, rinsed, drained, and picked over
- 1 whole clove
- 1 large onion, peeled but left whole
- 1 bay leaf
- 1 fresh thyme sprig
- 1 teaspoon salt
- 8 ounces sliced bacon
- ¼ cup finely chopped shallots
- 1 garlic clove, minced
- 1 cup heavy cream
- ¼ cup chopped fresh flat-leaf parsley

Place the lentils in a large slow cooker with water to cover by 1 inch. Stick the clove into the onion. Add the onion, bay leaf, thyme, and salt to the slow cooker. Cover and cook on low for 4 hours, or until the lentils are tender.

When the lentils are almost ready, place the bacon slices, overlapping slightly, in a large skillet. Cook over medium-high heat, turning the bacon occasionally, until crisp. Drain on paper towels.

Add the shallots and garlic to the skillet. Cook, stirring, over medium heat, for 2 minutes, or until the shallots are browned. Stir in the cream and cook, stirring, for 5 minutes, or until the cream is simmering and slightly thickened.

Drain the lentils well and discard the onion and herbs. Stir the cream sauce into the lentils. Chop the bacon. Sprinkle the lentils with the bacon and parsley and serve hot.

Giant Beans in Tomato Sauce

GREECE

Gigantes, or "giant beans," are large white beans similar to large limas, which are a good substitute. In this recipe, the beans are cooked Greek-style in a flavorful tomato sauce with vegetables and finished with tangy feta cheese. Serve the beans as they are or use them as a topping for cooked pasta.

SERVES 8

- 1 pound dried gigantes or large lima beans, rinsed, drained, and picked over
- 2 tablespoons olive oil
- 2 large onions, chopped
- 2 celery ribs, chopped
- 2 medium carrots, peeled and chopped
- 3 large garlic cloves, finely chopped
- 4 tablespoons tomato paste
- Salt and freshly ground pepper
- 7 cups water
- Pinch of crushed red pepper
- 1 bay leaf
- 1 teaspoon dried oregano
- ½ teaspoon dried thyme
- 1 cup crumbled feta cheese
- ¼ cup finely chopped fresh flat-leaf parsley

Place the beans in a large bowl with cold water to cover by several inches. Let stand at room temperature for 6 hours or in the refrigerator overnight.

In a large skillet, heat the oil over medium heat. Add the onions, celery, and carrots and cook, stirring occasionally, until tender, about 10 minutes. Stir in the garlic and cook for 1 minute. Add the tomato paste, 1 teaspoon salt, and pepper to taste. Add the water, crushed red pepper, bay leaf, oregano, and thyme. Bring the mixture to a simmer. Pour it into a large slow cooker.

Drain the beans and place them in the slow cooker. Cover and cook on low for 6 to 8 hours, or until the beans are very tender. Taste for seasonings.

Just before serving, discard the bay leaf. If there is too much liquid, mash some of the beans into the sauce. Stir in the cheese. Sprinkle with the parsley and serve hot.

Fava Bean Puree

Mashed dried fava beans have been a simple dietary staple of people throughout the Mediterranean for aeons. Until the discovery of the Americas, favas were the only form of beans that were grown in Europe and Asia.

In southern Italy, fava beans are cooked and mashed to a thick puree and served with a topping of sautéed bitter greens. In Lebanon they are seasoned with parsley, garlic, and hot sauce. In Egypt they are eaten as breakfast food, served with garnishes of hard-cooked eggs, pickles, or tomato and cucumber salad. Syrians eat the beans with yogurt, sesame paste, sheep's-milk cheese, and olives.

I like to serve them with a variety of toppings, according to the season. With pita bread, they make a delicious first course before a roast leg of lamb or an all-in-one meatless meal.

Peeled dried favas cook more quickly and are more digestible than the skin-on favas. Look for them in Middle Eastern and Italian markets. If you can find only the unpeeled beans, soak them overnight and cook them as in the recipe for Basic Chickpeas (page 175).

SERVES 8

1 pound peeled dried fava beans, rinsed, drained, and picked over

4 garlic cloves, peeled and left whole

Salt

1 teaspoon ground cumin

¼ cup fresh lemon juice

¼ cup extra-virgin olive oil

Freshly ground pepper

Crushed red pepper

Chopped tomatoes, chopped cucumbers, chopped red onions, chopped fresh cilantro, feta cheese, and olives

Pita bread

Place the beans in a large slow cooker. Add water to cover by 1 inch. Add 2 of the garlic cloves and 1 teaspoon salt. Cover and cook on high for 6 hours, or until the beans are tender.

Drain the beans, reserving the cooking liquid. Place the beans in a blender or food processor. Add the remaining 2 garlic cloves and puree until smooth. Add the cumin, lemon juice, oil, and salt and pepper to taste. If the puree is too thick, add some of the reserved cooking liquid.

Spread the bean puree on a large platter. Sprinkle with crushed red pepper to taste.

Toss together the tomatoes, cucumbers, onions, and cilantro and spoon it over the puree. Crumble the cheese and scatter it over the top, along with the olives. Serve with pita bread for dipping.

Vegetables

Vegetables

Roasted Beets

Here's a basic recipe for roasting beets in a slow cooker. The cooker acts like an oven, and the beets turn out uniformly tender and sweet. When trimming them, leave the roots attached so that they retain their juices. You can serve the beets on their own, use them for Beet and Goat Cheese Dip (page 188), or cut them into bite-size pieces and serve with a vinaigrette dressing.

SERVES 6

    Olive oil for the insert
6–8 medium to large beets (about 2 pounds), scrubbed

Oil the insert of a large slow cooker. Remove all but 1 inch of the beet tops. Leave the roots intact.

Place the beets in the cooker. Cover and cook on high for 3 to 4 hours, or until the beets are tender when pierced with a knife.

Remove the beets from the cooker and let cool slightly. With a small knife, peel off the skins and serve or use in another recipe (see headnote).

OUT OF THE POT *Beet and Goat Cheese Dip*

TURKEY

Yogurt, goat cheese, and roasted beets make a gorgeous fuchsia pink spread to serve on pita bread or as a dip with crackers.

MAKES 2 CUPS

½ cup plain Greek-style yogurt

⅓ cup soft goat cheese (about 3 ounces)

1 tablespoon extra-virgin olive oil

1 large garlic clove, very finely chopped or grated

½ teaspoon ground cumin

Salt

3–4 Roasted Beets (page 187), coarsely chopped

In a large bowl, mash together the yogurt and goat cheese. Blend in the olive oil, garlic, cumin, and salt to taste.

Stir the beets into the yogurt mixture. Serve slightly chilled.

Cauliflower with Tomatoes and Feta

GREECE

Ordinary cauliflower is dressed up the Greek way, with sweet little tomatoes, salty black olives, and tangy feta cheese. For a simple dinner, serve with hot whole wheat pita bread and grilled lamb kebabs.

SERVES 4 TO 6

¼ cup olive oil, plus more for the insert

2 cups halved cherry tomatoes or chopped tomatoes

½ cup water

1 cup halved pitted kalamata olives

2 garlic cloves, finely chopped

½ teaspoon dried oregano

Salt and freshly ground pepper

1 large cauliflower (about 2 pounds), trimmed and cut into 1-inch florets

½ cup crumbled feta cheese or grated sheep's milk cheese

Oil the insert of a large slow cooker. Place the tomatoes, water, olives, garlic, oregano, a pinch each of salt and pepper, and the ¼ cup oil in the cooker and stir. (Don't add too much salt because the olives may be salty.) Add the cauliflower and spoon the mixture over the florets. Cover and cook on high for 1½ hours, or until almost tender.

Sprinkle with the feta. Cover and cook on high for 30 minutes more. Serve hot or at room temperature.

Braised Green Beans with Bacon

FRANCE

I first tasted beans cooked this way at a simple country restaurant in Provence, where they were served alongside roasted pork ribs. They go well with roasted chicken too. With some good bread, I can make a meal of them.

SERVES 8

- 8 ounces sliced bacon, cut into ½-inch pieces
- 1 large onion, chopped
- 1 garlic clove, minced
- 1 large fresh tomato, chopped, or 1 cup chopped canned tomatoes
- 1 pound carrots, peeled and cut into ⅛-inch-thick slices
- 2 pounds green or wax beans, trimmed
  Pinch of salt
- 1 cup chicken or vegetable broth

In a large skillet, cook the bacon over medium heat for 12 minutes, or until it is golden brown and slightly crisp. Remove the bacon with a slotted spoon.

Add the onion to the skillet and cook, stirring occasionally, until it is tender and golden, about 10 minutes. Stir in the garlic and tomato and remove from the heat.

Place the carrot slices in a large slow cooker. Add the beans and salt.

Put half of the bacon on top, then add the tomato mixture and the broth.

Cover and cook on low for 5 to 6 hours or on high for 3 to 4 hours, or until the vegetables are tender. Stir in the remaining bacon. Serve hot.

Warm Potato Salad with Hot Pepper, Garlic, and Cilantro

LEBANON

The lively flavors of garlic, cilantro, and lemon juice in this potato salad will brighten any barbecue menu. Try it with grilled fish, lamb chops, or sausages.

SERVES 6

- 6 tablespoons olive oil, plus more for the insert
- 2 pounds Yukon Gold or other boiling potatoes, cut into ½-inch-thick slices
- Salt
- 1 cup chopped fresh cilantro
- 2 tablespoons finely chopped or grated garlic
- ½ teaspoon crushed red pepper
- 1–2 tablespoons fresh lemon juice
- 1 lemon, cut into wedges

Oil the insert of a large slow cooker. Add the potatoes, 2 tablespoons of the olive oil, and 1 teaspoon salt and toss well. Cover and cook on high for 3 to 4 hours, or until the potatoes are tender when pierced with a fork.

Warm the remaining ¼ cup oil over medium heat in a medium skillet. Add the cilantro, garlic, and crushed red pepper and cook for 2 to 3 minutes, or until fragrant. Remove from the heat and stir in 1 tablespoon of the lemon juice.

Pour the sauce over the potatoes and toss well. Taste for seasonings and add more lemon juice if desired. Serve warm, garnished with lemon wedges.

Lemon Potatoes with Oregano and Dill

GREECE

Oregano and dill, along with lemon juice, are typical flavorings in many Greek recipes. I like to serve these potatoes with grilled fish or lamb.

SERVES 6 TO 8

- ¼ cup olive oil, plus more for the insert
- 2 pounds boiling potatoes, such as Yukon Gold, cut into 1-inch chunks
- 1 large onion, chopped
- 2 garlic cloves, minced
- 1½ teaspoons dried oregano
- ½ teaspoon grated lemon zest
- Salt and freshly ground pepper
- 2–3 tablespoons fresh lemon juice
- 3 tablespoons chopped fresh dill

Oil the insert of a large slow cooker. Place the potatoes, onion, garlic, ¼ cup oil, oregano, lemon zest, 1 teaspoon salt, and pepper to taste in the cooker and toss well. Cover and cook on high for 3 hours, or until the potatoes are tender when pierced with a knife.

Transfer the potatoes to a serving bowl and toss with the lemon juice. Taste for seasonings. Sprinkle with the dill and serve hot.

Creamy Whipped Potatoes

FRANCE

I wouldn't suggest making mashed potatoes in the slow cooker for just two to four people, but when you need a big batch, this is a great way to go. The potatoes simmer in the slow cooker until tender, then are mashed with butter and cream—I use a wire whisk. If you use an electric mixer, don't overbeat the potatoes, or they will become gluey. Once they are mashed, scoop the potatoes back into the cooker to keep warm on low until you are ready to eat.

SERVES 12 TO 16

- 4 pounds russet (baking) potatoes, peeled and halved
- 1 garlic clove
- Salt
- ½ cup heavy cream or crème fraîche, heated
- ⅓ cup unsalted butter, softened
- Freshly ground pepper

Place the potatoes in a large slow cooker. Smash the garlic clove with the side of a chef's knife and add it to the potatoes. Add 1 teaspoon salt and enough water to just cover the potatoes.

Cover and cook on high for 3 to 4 hours, or until the potatoes are completely tender. With a slotted spoon, transfer them to a large bowl. Reserve ½ cup of the cooking water. Mash the potatoes until smooth with a potato masher or a sturdy wire whisk.

Beat in the cream, butter, and salt and pepper to taste. If the potatoes seem dry, stir in a little of the reserved cooking water. Serve hot.

Variations

- Stir in freshly grated Gruyère or Parmigiano-Reggiano.

- Stir in minced fresh chives or another herb.

- Substitute extra-virgin olive oil for the butter and use broth instead of cream.

Green Bean, Potato, and Tomato Stew

GREECE

There are many similarities between southern Italian and Greek cooking. This stew, known as *fasolakia* in Greece, reminds me of one my Sicilian aunt used to make, except she added some Italian-style pork sausages to the pot with the vegetables.

I like to make this delicious stew in the summertime, when green beans, potatoes, and tomatoes are at their flavor peak. If I have it, I stir in a tablespoon or so of fresh oregano or basil at the end of the cooking time.

SERVES 8

2	tablespoons olive oil, plus more for the insert
2	medium onions, chopped
2	garlic cloves, finely chopped
6	medium boiling potatoes, such as Yukon Gold, peeled and cut into ½-inch dice
1	pound green beans or Roma beans, trimmed
2	large fresh tomatoes, chopped, or 2 cups chopped canned tomatoes with their liquid
1	medium red bell pepper, chopped
	Salt and freshly ground pepper
½	cup chopped fresh flat-leaf parsley
1–2	tablespoons chopped fresh oregano or basil (optional)

Oil the insert of a large slow cooker.

Heat the 2 tablespoons oil in a medium skillet. Add the onions and cook over medium heat, stirring occasionally, until the onions are tender, about 10 minutes. Add the garlic and cook for 1 minute more.

Scatter the potatoes in the cooker. Add the green beans, tomatoes, bell pepper, and salt and pepper to taste. Add the contents of the skillet and toss well. Cover and cook on high for 2 to 3 hours, or until the vegetables are tender.

Sprinkle with the parsley and the oregano, if using. Serve hot or at room temperature.

Golden Vegetable Tagine

MOROCCO

The warm, sunny colors of this Moroccan-style tagine make it perfect for a hearty winter meal. Serve it as a main course over rice or couscous or as a side dish with grilled lamb chops or chicken.

SERVES 6 TO 8

- 2 tablespoons olive oil
- 2 medium onions, chopped
- 6 medium carrots, peeled and quartered
- 1 pound rutabaga, peeled and cut into 1-inch chunks
- 2 cups 1-inch chunks peeled butternut squash
- 12 dried apricots, halved
- 1 tablespoon freshly grated ginger
   Salt
- 1 teaspoon ground cumin
- ½ teaspoon ground cinnamon
- ¼ teaspoon cayenne pepper
- 2 cups Chicken Broth (page 44), Vegetable Broth (page 45), or store-bought broth
- ½ cup chopped fresh cilantro, mint, or flat-leaf parsley

Heat the oil in a medium skillet. Add the onions and cook, stirring occasionally, until they are tender, about 10 minutes.

Scrape the onions into a large slow cooker. Add 1 teaspoon salt and the remaining ingredients, except the herbs, and toss well. Cover and cook on low for 6 to 8 hours, or until the vegetables are tender.

Taste for seasonings. Sprinkle with the herbs and serve hot.

Tzimmes
(Sweet Potato and Fruit Casserole)

ISRAEL

Although probably of Eastern European origin, this simple fruit and vegetable casserole is a favorite on the table during Israeli holidays. Some cooks add pineapple or raisins, while others include ground cinnamon, and all the variations taste good. I like to serve the dish with roast chicken or fish, and it's great with braised beef brisket.

SERVES 6

- 6 medium sweet potatoes (about 3 pounds), peeled and cut into 1-inch wedges
- 1 pound carrots, peeled and cut into ½-inch-thick slices
- 1 cup quartered dried apricots
- 1 cup pitted prunes
- 1 cup orange juice
- ½ cup water
- 3 tablespoons honey
- 1 tablespoon freshly grated ginger
- Salt
- 2 tablespoons unsalted butter
- 1 teaspoon grated lemon zest

In a large slow cooker, combine the sweet potatoes, carrots, apricots, and prunes. Stir together the juice, water, honey, ginger, and 1 teaspoon salt in a small bowl. Pour the mixture over the vegetables and fruit. Cover and cook on low for 3 to 4 hours, or until the vegetables are tender.

Uncover and gently stir in the butter. Taste for seasoning. Sprinkle with the lemon zest and serve hot.

All-Purpose Tomato Sauce

Along with containers of homemade broth or packages of dried beans, this flavor-packed tomato sauce is something I always keep on hand. I use it for everything from pasta and polenta to omelets, rice, meat loaf, fish, and pizza.

Since I use canned tomatoes, I can make this sauce year-round. The consistency is just right, neither too thick nor too thin, which comes from the combination of whole and crushed tomatoes. Celery, carrots, and onions give the sauce natural sweetness and a little texture. I add the butter or oil at the end of the cooking time so that I can taste their rich flavor more clearly. The sauce freezes well too.

MAKES ABOUT 10 CUPS

- 2 **28-ounce cans tomatoes, chopped, with their juice**
- 1 **28-ounce can crushed tomatoes**
- 2 **large carrots, peeled and chopped**
- 2 **celery ribs, chopped**
- 2 **medium onions, chopped**
- 2 **garlic cloves, chopped**
- 1 **bay leaf**
  Salt and freshly ground pepper
- 8 **tablespoons (1 stick) unsalted butter or ½ cup extra-virgin olive oil**

In a large slow cooker, combine the tomatoes, carrots, celery, onions, garlic, bay leaf, 1 teaspoon salt, and pepper to taste. Cover and cook on low for 5 hours, or until the vegetables are tender.

Let cool slightly. Discard the bay leaf. Pour the sauce into a food processor and process until smooth or use an immersion blender. Reheat if needed. Stir in the butter. Taste for seasonings.

Use immediately or freeze in small airtight containers for up to 3 months.

Variation

- Stir in 2 tablespoons chopped fresh flat-leaf parsley or basil or ½ teaspoon dried oregano along with the butter.

Desserts

Desserts

Bittersweet Cocoa Almond Cake

SPAIN

This Spanish cake is made with cocoa, not chocolate. The color is practically black, the texture dense, and the flavor bittersweet. It tastes rich, but it's actually much lower in fat than similar flourless cakes that contain chocolate.

For the best flavor, use Dutch-process cocoa. When you cut the cake, dip the knife into a glass of cool water between cuts so that it will glide smoothly through the soft cake.

SERVES 8

- 4 tablespoons (½ stick) unsalted butter, melted and cooled, plus more for the pan
- ½ cup whole almonds (with skins), lightly toasted
- 1¼ cups Dutch-process cocoa
- 1 cup water
- 1 teaspoon vanilla extract
- ¾ cup sugar
- 3 large eggs, plus 2 large egg whites
  Pinch of salt
- 2 tablespoons sliced almonds (with skins)
  Whipped cream

Butter a 6-cup soufflé dish. Line the bottom of the dish with wax paper and butter the paper. Place a rack in a large slow cooker.

Place the whole almonds in a food processor fitted with the steel blade. Process until finely ground. Remove from the processor.

Put the cocoa, water, and vanilla into the processor and process until smooth. Add the 4 tablespoons melted butter and ½ cup of the sugar and mix well, about 30 seconds. With the machine running, add the whole eggs, one at a time, and process until smooth, about 30 seconds more. Stir in the ground almonds.

In a large bowl, with an electric mixer, beat the egg whites and the salt on medium speed until light and fluffy. Increase the speed to high and beat in the remaining ¼ cup sugar until soft peaks form, about 3 minutes. Fold the cocoa mixture into the egg white mixture. Scrape the batter into the prepared dish.

Place the dish on the rack in the slow cooker. Carefully pour hot water to a depth of about 1 inch around the outside of the dish. Cover and cook on high for 2½ hours, or until just set. The center will look a little wet, but that's OK.

Protecting your hands with oven mitts, carefully remove the dish from the cooker. Place it on a rack and let cool for 20 minutes.

Run a knife around the edge of the cake. Invert the cake onto a serving plate. Peel off the wax paper. Cover with an inverted bowl and refrigerate for several hours or overnight.

Just before serving, sprinkle the cake with the sliced almonds. Cut into slices and serve with whipped cream.

Apricot Almond Cake

ITALY

I adapted this recipe from my book *La Dolce Vita*, about home-style Italian desserts. With a slice of this cake and a cup of cappuccino, you'll feel as if you are enjoying *la dolce vita* in Italy.

The cake is packed with toasted almonds and topped with a shiny bright glaze of apricot jam and sliced almonds. Although it's simple to make, it's quite glamorous and worthy of a special occasion.

SERVES 8

- 4 tablespoons (½ stick) unsalted butter, softened, plus more for the pan
- 1 cup whole almonds (with skins), toasted
- 1 cup sugar
- ½ cup all-purpose flour
- ¼ teaspoon baking powder
- 4 large eggs, at room temperature
- 1 teaspoon vanilla extract
- ¼ teaspoon almond extract

APRICOT GLAZE

- ⅓ cup apricot jam
- 2 tablespoons sugar
- 2–3 tablespoons sliced almonds (with skins), toasted

Butter a 7-x-2-inch round cake pan or a 6-cup soufflé dish. Line the bottom of the pan with wax paper and butter the paper. Place a rack in a large slow cooker. Pour 2 cups hot water into the cooker and turn on the cooker.

In a food processor or blender, combine the whole almonds and ¼ cup of the sugar. Process just until very finely ground, about 1 minute. Add the flour and baking powder and pulse 2 or 3 times to blend.

In a large bowl with an electric mixer, beat the 4 tablespoons butter and the remaining ¾ cup sugar on medium speed until very light and fluffy. Beat in the eggs, one at a time, until smooth and well blended. Scrape down the sides of the bowl. Beat in the vanilla and almond extracts.

With a rubber spatula, fold in the ground almond mixture. Scrape the batter into the prepared pan.

Place the cake pan on the rack in the slow cooker. Cover and cook on high for 3 hours, or until a toothpick inserted into the center comes out clean.

Protecting your hands with oven mitts, carefully remove the pan from the cooker. Place it on a rack and let cool for 10 minutes. Run a knife around the edge of the cake. Invert the cake onto a wire rack. Peel off the wax paper. Let the cake cool completely.

MAKE THE APRICOT GLAZE: Heat the jam and sugar in a small saucepan over medium heat. When the mixture starts to simmer, stir well until melted. Strain the glaze through a fine-mesh sieve into a small bowl, pressing on the solids.

Pour the glaze onto the top of the cake and spread it smooth. Sprinkle the sliced almonds in a border around the top edge of the cake. Let cool before serving.

Walnut Cake with Cinnamon Syrup

GREECE

A cinnamon-flavored syrup keeps this walnut-packed cake moist. Add a table-spoon or so of Greek brandy to the finished syrup if you like. The cake is perfect as is, but if you happen to have some coffee ice cream on hand, they're great together.

SERVES 8

    Unsalted butter for the pan
1 **cup toasted walnuts**
½ **cup sugar**
½ **cup all-purpose flour**
1 **teaspoon baking powder**
1 **teaspoon ground cinnamon**
½ **teaspoon grated lemon zest**
    Pinch of salt
2 **large eggs, plus 1 large egg yolk**
½ **cup plain Greek-style yogurt**
¼ **cup olive oil**

CINNAMON SYRUP

1 **cup sugar**
½ **cup water**
1 **3-inch cinnamon stick**
1 **2-inch strip lemon zest**

Butter a 7-x-2-inch round cake pan or a 6-cup soufflé dish. Line the bottom of the pan with wax paper and butter the paper. Place a rack in a large slow cooker. Pour 2 cups hot water into the cooker, and turn on the cooker.

In a food processor or blender, combine the walnuts and ¼ cup of the sugar. Process until very finely ground, about 1 minute. Add the flour, baking powder, ground cinnamon, lemon zest, and salt. Pulse 2 or 3 times to blend.

In another bowl, whisk together the whole eggs, the egg yolk, the remaining ¼ cup sugar, the yogurt, and olive oil. Stir in the dry ingredients. Scrape the batter into the prepared pan. Place the cake pan on the rack in the slow cooker. Cover and cook on high for 2¼ hours, or until a knife inserted into the center comes out clean.

Protecting your hands with oven mitts, carefully remove the pan from the cooker. Place it on a rack and let cool for 10 minutes. Run a knife around the edge of the cake. Invert the cake onto a wire rack. Remove the wax paper. Let the cake cool completely.

MAKE THE CINNAMON SYRUP: In a small saucepan, combine all the syrup ingredients. Bring to a simmer and cook, stirring occasionally, for 10 minutes, or until slightly thickened. Let cool.

Slide the cake onto a serving dish. Remove the cinnamon stick and the lemon zest from the syrup. Pour the syrup over the cake. Let stand for at least 1 hour before serving so that the cake can absorb some of the syrup.

Sunny Orange Cake
with Orange Syrup

GREECE

This orange cake is made with semolina, a kind of coarse flour that comes from durum wheat. It is the same thing as my childhood favorite breakfast cereal, farina. It gives this cake a slightly grainy and spongy texture—the perfect vehicle for the orangey syrup.

The bright flavor of this cake is especially welcome on a gloomy day, and a dollop of whipped cream makes it even better.

SERVES 8

- 4 tablespoons (½ stick) unsalted butter, softened, plus more for the pan
- ½ cup all-purpose flour
- ½ cup fine semolina or farina
- 1 teaspoon baking powder
- ½ cup sugar
- 2 large eggs, separated
- 1 teaspoon vanilla extract
- ½ teaspoon grated orange zest
- ½ cup whole milk
- Pinch of salt

ORANGE SYRUP

- ¾ cup sugar
- ¾ cup orange juice
- ½ teaspoon grated orange zest
- Fresh orange slices and mint leaves

Place a rack in a large slow cooker. Butter a 7-x-2-inch round cake pan. Line the bottom of the pan with wax paper and butter the paper.

Stir together the flour, semolina, and baking powder. In a large bowl with an electric mixer, beat the 4 tablespoons butter and the sugar on medium speed

until light and fluffy, about 2 minutes. Add the egg yolks and beat until light, about 3 minutes. Beat in the vanilla and orange zest. Add the flour mixture in 3 additions, alternating with the milk and beginning and ending with the flour.

In a medium bowl with clean beaters, beat the egg whites and the salt on medium speed until soft peaks form. Gently fold the egg whites into the semolina mixture. Scrape the mixture into the prepared pan.

Place the pan on the rack in the slow cooker. Pour hot water around the cake pan to a depth of 1 inch. Cover and cook on high for 2 to 2½ hours, or until the cake starts to pull away from the side of the pan and a knife inserted into the center comes out clean.

Protecting your hands with oven mitts, carefully remove the pan from the slow cooker. Place on a rack and let cool for 10 minutes. Run a knife around the edge of the cake. Invert the cake onto a wire rack. Remove the wax paper. Let the cake cool completely.

MAKE THE ORANGE SYRUP: Combine the sugar and orange juice in a small saucepan. Bring the mixture to a simmer and stir until the sugar is dissolved, about 5 minutes. Stir in the orange zest. Remove from the heat and let cool.

Slowly pour the orange syrup over the cake. Let stand for at least 1 hour so that the cake can absorb some of the syrup. Garnish with the orange slices and mint leaves. Cut into slices and serve.

Two-Berry Clafouti

FRANCE

A clafouti is a soft pudding cake that you can whip up in a jiffy with all kinds of soft or cooked fruits. Well-drained canned or thawed frozen fruits work too. This version is perfect for the summertime, when fresh berries are plentiful. It's great for breakfast with some Greek-style yogurt or for dessert with ice cream. I like it best at room temperature.

SERVES 4 TO 6

- 2 cups fresh blueberries, rinsed and patted dry, or thawed frozen, drained
- 1 cup fresh raspberries, rinsed and patted dry, or thawed frozen, drained
- 1 3-ounce package cream cheese, softened
- ½ cup sugar
- 3 large eggs
- ½ cup milk
- ½ teaspoon grated lemon or orange zest
- ¼ cup all-purpose flour
  Confectioners' sugar for sprinkling

Spray the insert of a large slow cooker with nonstick cooking spray. Scatter the berries in the slow cooker.

In a blender, combine the cream cheese and sugar. Add the eggs, milk, and zest and blend well. Add the flour and blend until smooth, about 1 minute. Pour the mixture over the berries.

Cover and cook on high for 1½ to 2 hours, or until the clafouti is slightly puffed and the center jiggles slightly when the sides are tapped.

Allow to cool to room temperature. Scoop onto serving plates and serve, sprinkled with confectioners' sugar.

Cannoli Cheesecake

ITALY

News flash: slow cookers can't do everything! One day, I was craving cannoli, the crisp pastry tubes filled with luscious whipped ricotta flavored with chocolate, orange, and pistachio that are a favorite dessert in Sicily. I came up with the next best thing—this easy cheesecake. True, it does not have the crunchy fried crust of genuine cannoli, but the flavor is completely irresistible.

Whole-milk ricotta has the right creamy texture you need for this cake, and miniature chocolate chips hold their shape well. Depending on the brand of ricotta used, the chips may stay suspended or sink and form a chocolaty layer on the bottom; either way is great.

SERVES 8

Unsalted butter for the pan

1 15- to 16-ounce container whole-milk ricotta

6 ounces cream cheese, softened

⅔ cup confectioners' sugar

½ teaspoon ground cinnamon

1 teaspoon vanilla extract

2 large eggs

½ cup miniature semisweet chocolate chips

2 tablespoons chopped candied orange peel or 1 teaspoon grated orange zest

½ cup coarsely chopped unsalted pistachios

Place a rack in a large slow cooker. Butter a 7-inch springform pan. Place the pan in the center of a large sheet of aluminum foil and wrap the foil around the sides so that water cannot enter.

In a food processor, beat the ricotta and cream cheese with the confectioners' sugar, cinnamon, and vanilla until very smooth, about 5 minutes. Add the eggs and process until blended, about 2 minutes. With a spoon, lightly stir in the chocolate chips and candied orange peel. Pour the mixture into the prepared pan.

Pour hot water to a depth of about 1 inch around the pan. Cover and cook on high for 2½ hours, or until the cheesecake is set around the edges yet soft and jiggly in the center. Protecting your hands with oven mitts, carefully remove the pan from the cooker and let cool slightly on a rack. Cover and refrigerate for at least 2 hours or overnight.

Run a knife around the edge of the cheesecake. Remove the sides of the pan. Press the pistachios onto the sides of the cake. Cut into wedges and serve.

Chocolate Hazelnut Cheesecake

ITALY

Italians are crazy about the combination of hazelnuts and chocolate known as gianduja. There are gianduja chocolate bars, ice cream, sauces, and cakes, but the most popular version of this suave flavor combo is the smooth, creamy spread sold under the brand name Nutella. Kids and adults alike eat it on toast for breakfast, spread it on cookies for a snack, and even stuff it into hot pizza crust for dessert. Nutella is pretty popular here, too, and is widely available in supermarkets, though there are other brands on the market.

Inspired by a version I had in Italy, I came up with this luscious cheesecake, a must for Nutella fans.

SERVES 8

> 3 tablespoons unsalted butter, melted, plus more for the pan
>
> ⅔ cup chocolate wafer cookie crumbs
>
> 1 15- to 16-ounce container whole-milk ricotta
>
> ⅔ cup Nutella or other chocolate hazelnut spread
>
> ¼ cup sugar
>
> 2 large eggs

Place a rack in a large slow cooker. Butter a 7-inch springform pan. Place the pan in the center of a large sheet of aluminum foil and wrap the foil around the sides so that water cannot enter.

In a small bowl, stir together the cookie crumbs and the 3 tablespoons melted butter. Press the mixture firmly into the base of the prepared pan. Place the pan in the refrigerator.

In a food processor or with a hand mixer, beat the ricotta and Nutella with the sugar until very smooth, about 2 minutes. Add the eggs, one at a time, and process until blended, stopping once or twice to scrape down the sides of the bowl. Pour the mixture into the pan.

Place the pan on the rack in the slow cooker. Pour hot water to a depth of about 1 inch around the pan. Cover and cook on high for 2½ hours, or until the cheesecake is set around the edges yet soft and jiggly in the center.

Protecting your hands with oven mitts, carefully remove the pan from the slow cooker and let cool slightly on a rack. Cover and refrigerate for at least 2 hours or overnight.

Run a knife around the edge of the cheesecake. Remove the sides of the pan. Cut into wedges and serve.

Coffee Caramel Flan

SPAIN

With its smooth, creamy texture and sophisticated flavor, this flan is right for any occasion. Canned sweetened condensed milk and evaporated milk are convenient to have in the pantry so that you can put this flan together anytime.

SERVES 8

- 1 cup sugar
- ¼ cup water
- 1 12-ounce can evaporated milk
- 1 14-ounce can sweetened condensed milk
- 2 large eggs, plus 2 large egg yolks
- 2 tablespoons instant espresso powder dissolved in 1 tablespoon hot water

Place a rack in a large slow cooker.

In a small saucepan, combine the sugar and water. Cook over medium heat, swirling the pan occasionally, until the sugar is dissolved, about 5 minutes. Simmer the mixture without stirring until it begins to turn brown around the edges, about 10 minutes. Gently swirl the pan until the syrup is evenly caramelized.

Protecting your hand with an oven mitt, pour the hot syrup into a 6-cup soufflé dish, turning the dish to coat the bottom evenly. Let cool until the caramel is just set.

In a medium bowl, whisk together the evaporated milk and condensed milk. Beat in the eggs, yolks, and espresso until blended. Pour the mixture into the soufflé dish.

Place the dish on the rack in the slow cooker. Pour hot water to a depth of 1 inch around the soufflé dish. Cover and cook on high for 2 to 2½ hours, until a knife inserted near the center comes out clean.

Protecting your hands with oven mitts, carefully remove the dish from the slow cooker. Let cool slightly, then cover and refrigerate until chilled, several hours or overnight.

Run a knife around the inside of the dish. Invert a serving plate on top of the dish and quickly invert the two. Carefully remove the dish, allowing the caramel to drizzle over the cream. Cut into wedges and serve.

Coconut Flan

SPAIN

You will find smooth, creamy custard topped with liquid caramel under a variety of names in many places throughout the world, not just in the Mediterranean. This coconut version is one of my favorites.

SERVES 8

- ½ cup sugar
- ¼ cup water
- 1 12-ounce can evaporated milk
- 1 15-ounce can cream of coconut
- 4 large eggs
- 1 tablespoon brandy or rum or 1 teaspoon vanilla extract

Place a rack in a large slow cooker.

In a small saucepan, combine the sugar and water. Cook over medium heat, swirling the pan occasionally, until the sugar is dissolved, about 5 minutes. Simmer the mixture without stirring until it begins to turn brown around the edges, about 10 minutes. Gently swirl the pan until the syrup is evenly caramelized.

Protecting your hand with an oven mitt, pour the hot syrup into a 6-cup soufflé dish, turning the dish to coat the bottom evenly. Let cool until the caramel is just set.

In a medium bowl, whisk together the evaporated milk and cream of coconut. Beat in the eggs and brandy until blended. Pour the mixture into the soufflé dish.

Place the dish on the rack in the slow cooker. Pour hot water to a depth of 1 inch around the soufflé dish. Cover and cook on high for 3 to 3½ hours, until the flan is set around the edges and slightly soft in the center. It will thicken as it cools.

Protecting your hands with oven mitts, carefully remove the dish from the slow cooker. Let cool slightly, then cover and refrigerate until chilled, several hours or overnight.

Run a knife around the inside of the dish. Invert a serving plate on top of the dish and quickly invert the two. Carefully remove the dish, allowing the caramel to drizzle over the cream. Cut into wedges and serve.

Lemon Cheese Flan

FRANCE

When raspberries or strawberries are in season, I arrange them on a plate beside this luxurious flan flavored with lemon and cream cheese. I like to serve it after a springtime fish dinner.

SERVES 8

- 1½ cups sugar
- ¼ cup water
- 1 8-ounce package cream cheese, softened
- 1 12-ounce can evaporated milk
- 3 large eggs
- 1 teaspoon grated lemon zest
- 1 teaspoon vanilla extract

Place a rack in a large slow cooker.

In a small saucepan, combine 1 cup of the sugar and the water. Cook over medium heat, swirling the pan occasionally, until the sugar is dissolved, about 5 minutes. Simmer the mixture without stirring until it begins to turn brown around the edges, about 10 minutes. Gently swirl the pan until the syrup is evenly caramelized.

Protecting your hand with an oven mitt, pour the hot syrup into a 6-cup soufflé dish, turning the dish to coat the bottom evenly. Let cool until the caramel is just set.

In a large bowl, whisk together the remaining ½ cup sugar, the cream cheese, evaporated milk, eggs, lemon zest, and vanilla until blended. Pour the mixture into the soufflé dish.

Place the dish on the rack in the slow cooker. Pour hot water to a depth of 1 inch around the soufflé dish. Cover and cook on high for 2 to 2½ hours, or until a knife inserted near the center comes out clean.

Carefully remove the dish from the slow cooker. Let cool slightly, then cover and refrigerate until chilled, several hours or overnight.

Run a knife around the inside of the dish. Invert a serving plate on top of the dish and quickly invert the two. Carefully remove the dish, allowing the caramel to drizzle over the cream. Cut into wedges and serve.

Apple Raisin Soufflé Pudding

FRANCE

This recipe is made in two stages. First, you partially cook the apples and raisins. Then you make a soufflé-like batter and pour it over the fruit. This warm, comforting dessert is perfect for a chilly autumn day.

SERVES 8

6 large sweet apples, such as Golden Delicious, peeled and thinly sliced

1 cup golden raisins

¼ cup sugar

2 tablespoons unsalted butter, melted

1 teaspoon grated lemon zest

2 tablespoons all-purpose flour

2 tablespoons cognac or rum

TOPPING

8 tablespoons (1 stick) unsalted butter, softened

½ cup sugar

3 large eggs, separated

1 cup milk

2 tablespoons cognac or rum (optional)

½ cup all-purpose flour

Pinch of salt

Spray the insert of a large slow cooker with nonstick cooking spray. Add the apples, raisins, sugar, butter, lemon zest, flour, and cognac and toss well. Cover and cook on high for 1½ to 2 hours, or until the apples are softened but not quite tender.

MAKE THE TOPPING: When the apples are almost ready, beat the butter with the sugar with an electric mixer in a large bowl until light, about 3 minutes. Add the egg yolks and blend well. In a small bowl, stir together the milk and cognac, if using. Gently stir the milk mixture into the sugar mixture in 3 additions, alternating with the flour in 2 additions. The mixture may look curdled, but it will be fine.

In a large bowl with clean beaters, beat the egg whites and salt on medium speed until foamy. Continue beating until soft peaks form. Gently fold the egg whites into the yolk mixture.

Stir the apples. Scrape the topping over the apples. It's OK if some of the apples peek through the topping. Cover and cook on high for 1 hour, or until the topping is puffed and a knife inserted into the center comes out clean.

Uncover and remove the insert from the cooker. Let cool slightly.

Scoop the pudding onto serving plates and serve warm or at room temperature.

Pistachio and Golden Raisin Bread Pudding

MIDDLE EAST

Every Mediterranean meal includes bread, so often some is left over. That's the time to make bread pudding. This one captures the sweet flavors so typical of the Middle East. It's wonderful served either plain or with whipped cream or ice cream, but I like it for a special breakfast or brunch too, in which case, I top it with a scoop of creamy Greek-style yogurt.

Try figs, dates, or other dried fruits instead of the raisins, or almonds or pine nuts instead of the pistachios. Whole wheat bread is a nice change too.

SERVES 8

- 8 ounces French bread, torn into bite-size pieces and lightly toasted (about 6 cups)
- ½ cup golden raisins
- ½ cup unsalted pistachios
- 6 large eggs
- ½ cup sugar
- 1 teaspoon ground cinnamon
- ¼ cup honey
- 1 tablespoon grated orange zest
- 3 cups milk
- 1½ teaspoons vanilla extract

Spray the insert of a large slow cooker with nonstick cooking spray. Scatter the bread, raisins, and pistachios in the cooker.

In a large bowl, whisk the eggs until frothy. Beat in the sugar, cinnamon, honey, and orange zest. Stir in the milk and vanilla.

Pour the liquid over the bread mixture and stir.

Cover and cook on high for 2½ to 3 hours, or until the center is just barely set and slightly puffed. Uncover and remove the insert from the cooker. Let cool slightly. Scoop the pudding into bowls and serve warm.

White Chocolate Bread Pudding with Raspberried Strawberries

FRANCE

Even out-of-season strawberries take on a rich, sweet flavor when they are tossed with raspberry jam. I love to serve them on this soft, creamy French bread pudding flavored with white chocolate. I toast the bread first so some pieces rise to the surface and form a crunchy topping, but it is not essential if you are pressed for time.

SERVES 8

- 1 cup chopped white chocolate (10 ounces)
- 2 cups milk, heated until hot
- ⅔ cup sugar
- 1 cup heavy cream
- 4 large eggs, beaten
- 2 teaspoons vanilla extract
- 8 ounces brioche or challah bread, cut into 1-inch cubes and lightly toasted (about 6 cups)
- 1 pint strawberries, sliced
- 2–3 tablespoons seedless raspberry jam

Spray the insert of a large slow cooker with nonstick cooking spray.

Place the white chocolate in a large, heatproof bowl. Add the hot milk and sugar and let stand for 5 minutes. Stir until the white chocolate is melted and the sugar is dissolved. Whisk together the cream, eggs, and vanilla and stir the mixture into the white chocolate mixture.

Scatter the bread cubes in the slow cooker. Pour the white chocolate mixture over the bread. Cover and cook on high for 1 hour. Reduce the heat to low and cook for 1½ hours, or until the pudding is softly set in the center. Uncover and remove the insert from the cooker. Let cool slightly.

Meanwhile, toss the berries with the jam and let stand for 30 minutes, until juicy. Scoop the pudding into bowls. Top with the marinated strawberries and serve.

Rice Pudding Brûlée

Rice pudding with a hint of cinnamon and a crunchy caramelized sugar topping is a specialty of the Asturias region, on the northern coast of Spain. The pudding can be made ahead of time, but the topping needs to be added just before serving, or it will soon lose its crunch. If you are in a hurry, you can serve the pudding warm from the cooker without the topping.

SERVES 8

- 4 cups milk
- 1 cup heavy cream
- ¾ cup Arborio rice or another short-grain white rice
- 2 2-inch strips orange zest
- 1 3-inch cinnamon stick
- Pinch of salt
- 2 tablespoons brandy or 1 teaspoon vanilla extract
- ¾ cup sugar
- Pinch of ground cinnamon

Spray the insert of a large slow cooker with nonstick cooking spray.

Pour the milk and cream into the slow cooker. Stir in the rice, orange zest, cinnamon stick, and salt. Cover and cook on high for 2½ to 3 hours, stirring 2 or 3 times so that the rice doesn't stick to the bottom, until the rice is tender. Stir in the brandy and ½ cup of the sugar. Cover and cook for 20 minutes more, or until the sugar dissolves.

Remove the cinnamon stick and orange zest. Spread the pudding in a shallow, flameproof baking dish and smooth the top. The pudding will seem loose, but will firm up as it cools. Place a piece of plastic wrap directly on the surface of the pudding and refrigerate until completely cold, at least 2 hours or overnight.

Just before serving, position an oven rack about 3 inches from the broiler. Turn the broiler to high.

Remove the plastic wrap and place the dish on a baking sheet. Stir together the remaining ¼ cup sugar and the ground cinnamon. Sprinkle the mixture over the surface of the pudding. Place under the broiler for 2 to 3 minutes, or until the sugar is browned and bubbling. (Watch carefully so that it does not burn.) Remove the baking dish and let cool for 5 minutes before serving.

Blushing Pomegranate Pears

TURKEY

Pomegranates are plentiful in the Mediterranean, and you often find the trees growing in backyard gardens. The tart, sweet juice is now widely available in bottles. Mixed with seltzer, it makes a very refreshing drink, and I also like it for poaching fruit such as peeled pears, which turn a soft pink color as they cook.

SERVES 8

- ⅔ cup sugar
- 2 cups pomegranate juice
- 2 3-inch strips orange zest
- 10 whole black peppercorns
- 8 firm ripe pears, such as Bosc or Anjou, peeled
- 2 tablespoons chopped unsalted pistachios or sliced almonds

In a large slow cooker, stir together the sugar and juice. Add the orange zest and peppercorns.

Place the pears upright in the cooker and spoon some of the liquid over them. Cover and cook on high for 3 hours, or until the pears are tender when pierced with a knife.

Carefully transfer the pears to a serving dish. Strain the juices through a fine-mesh sieve into a small saucepan. Bring the juices to a simmer and cook until thickened and reduced slightly, about 5 minutes. Pour the syrup over the pears. Chill until serving time.

Just before serving, sprinkle the pears with the nuts.

Warm Fruit Compote with Mascarpone Sauce

MIDDLE EAST

My mother got the original recipe for this compote from a coworker, and it quickly became a family favorite. Over the years, I have tinkered with the ingredients. To dress it up, I top it with a luscious sauce made with mascarpone. A thick, slightly tangy Italian-style cream cheese, mascarpone is my first choice, but you can substitute crème fraîche or sour cream with delicious results.

Any leftover compote can be stored in the refrigerator for several days. Serve it on hot cereal, pancakes, or waffles for breakfast or on sliced pound cake for dessert.

SERVES 10 TO 12

- 3½ cups sweet wine, such as Asti Spumante or Moscato, or apple juice
- ½ cup sugar
- 1 cup halved dried apricots
- 1 cup dried figs
- 1 cup pitted prunes
- 1 cup muscat or golden raisins
- 1 cup dried cranberries
- ½ cup dried pitted cherries
- 1 cinnamon stick
- 1 3-inch strip orange zest

SAUCE

- 4 ounces mascarpone (½ cup)
- 1–2 tablespoons confectioners' sugar
- 1 tablespoon dark rum
- About ½ cup heavy cream

In a large slow cooker, combine the wine and sugar and stir well. Add the dried fruits, cinnamon, and orange zest. If necessary, add enough water so that the fruits are just covered with liquid. Cover and cook on high for 2 hours, or until the fruits are tender. Let cool slightly. Discard the cinnamon stick and orange zest.

MAKE THE SAUCE: Whisk together the mascarpone, sugar to taste, and rum. Gradually beat in the heavy cream until smooth.

Serve the fruit in goblets, drizzled with the sauce.

Index